The Learning Transformation

A GUIDE TO BLENDED LEARNING
FOR ADMINISTRATORS

The Learning Transformation

A GUIDE TO BLENDED LEARNING FOR ADMINISTRATORS

DEBB OLIVER

Gideon—
You are the
leader of the transformation!
Debb

LLP

LEAD+
LEARN
PRESS

ENGLEWOOD, COLORADO

The Leadership and Learning Center
5680 Greenwood Plaza Boulevard, Suite 550
Greenwood Village, Colorado 80111
Phone 1.866.399.6019 | Fax 303.504.9417
www.leadandlearn.com

Published by Lead + Learn Press.

ISBN 978-1-935588-46-7

Printed in the United States of America

01 02 03 04 05 06   20 19 18 17 16 15

4500520944   A B C D E F G

To my children,
who have inspired me;

and to their children,
whom we will all inspire.

Contents

Foreword

Mary Cullinane

There have been a lot of books written and a lot of promises made. We look all around us and things feel different. Information is more readily available. Communication is happening through tools and at speeds that we couldn't have even imagined fifteen years ago. Trends are measured in minutes rather than seasons. As a result, educators have been challenged to reflect these new norms in their classrooms. Many do, and do so well. Others struggle with the value of such "innovation." And others choose not to look. But there is no mistake. Things are different today, and we can be better.

What will this transformation look like in full practice? Where will this change ultimately bring us? My colleagues and I are in the midst of this evolving environment on a daily basis, thinking about the possibilities and challenges inherent in these and similar questions. The demand for innovative learning tools is growing, but technology—with all its potential—will never be the sole solution in accelerating learning and providing equal opportunities for all children.

As educators, content providers, and curriculum experts, we must work toward *a learning transformation, not a digital transformation.* A learning transformation means shifting our focus from "device first" to "learning first." Simply putting a tablet into the hands of a child isn't going to work. Adding an interactive whiteboard to the front of the classroom will not catapult reading scores.

As a community, we must ask tough questions and challenge ourselves. We must consider implementation processes and the technology-readiness levels of each school and district. We must think more about the connections between informal and formal learning experiences. We must define academic success by competency-based outcomes, not simply seat time, so that each learner is given the skills he or she needs to be truly successful.

When it comes to implementing technology, we need to focus on "learning first solutions." As we assess digital tools, we should ask ourselves whether the technology *enhances* the learning experience. Does it make content more engaging or effective? Does it create a productive environment for the instructor?

The pages to follow will help you answer these questions and more. Debb Oliver combines research and deep expertise with real-world application to illustrate a "learning first" model for integrating digital resources into your school. From leadership and decision making to ensuring appropriate infrastructure, *The Learning Transformation* is designed to support administrators and educators as they embark on building blended learning environments to fuel positive change.

All of us in the education space are uniquely positioned to make a difference and tackle the challenges at hand. We have the collective knowledge, capabilities, resources, and expertise to leverage technology in order to make learning more effective, dynamic, and fun. As long as we continue to make "learning first" our motto, the future looks brighter than ever. I can't wait to get there.

Mary Cullinane is Chief Content Officer
and Executive Vice President, Corporate
Affairs, at Houghton Mifflin Harcourt.

Acknowledgments

Over the years I have had the opportunity to work with educators in every U.S. state and in many other parts of the world. I have learned right alongside them, and have been inspired to help them take their passion and use it to guide their actions, in order to prepare our learners for the future.

I gratefully acknowledge the expertise of the team that helped write this book. Their contributions offer insights that are a result of their experience in their areas of expertise. Marge Fostiak, Ed.D., retired superintendent, has taken her district through the journey of digital transformation. Her innovative ideas paved the way for many districts to follow. Emerging onto the national stage, Weston Kieschnick brings his experience and insight as a teacher, coach, and administrator for online and blended schools. He is currently sharing his expertise with districts across the country as a Professional Development Associate with The Leadership and Learning Center. A Technology Director for many years, Julene Reed is also an Apple Distinguished Educator, Google Certified Instructor, and a member of the Discovery Education Leadership Council. A Fulbright Scholar, Denise Phillips has extensive classroom experience which has made her a teacher's teacher. She has an incredible ability to design curriculum and develop opportunities for teachers and administrators to learn effective strategies for integrating technology. I am indebted to these individuals for their prose and counsel.

I also have deep gratitude for the insightful and astute editorial eyes of Alan Bernhard and Carrie Williams at Lead + Learn Press. They have made this book a better one. For his never waning encouragement, I thank my husband, Doug.

Introduction

The world of education needs to catch up with ... the world. In recent decades we've grown accustomed to living in a world that is digitally connected, creative, and transforming before our eyes, yet somehow much of this transformation has remained outside the walls of our schools. In 1993, AT&T ran an ad campaign called "You Will," which prophetically showed what we would eventually be doing with technology in our daily lives, such as paying tolls without slowing down, unlocking doors with our voices, and making video phone calls. In 2011, a mere 18 years after that campaign, the New Media Consortium's *Horizon Report* gave a time frame of one year for mobile devices to be pervasive in the education setting. Can you imagine your life today without your mobile device?

While there have been many indicators that developing technologies would create critical change in education, the day-to-day operations of schools and districts have remained largely the same as they were in the late 1990s, when I was a classroom teacher.

Schools' efforts to incorporate technology have resulted in many disappointments. I witnessed computers being purchased and labs being organized, only to see them sit idle for the majority of the day. Schedules were not adjusted to accommodate the use of the labs, and many useful Web sites would be blocked by the district's filter, regardless of their educational application. Teachers were spending more time finding a workaround to access sites than they were planning or facilitating learning.

The interactive whiteboard was another tool that promised to change the way we teach. While students participated on interactive whiteboards in a few classrooms, I saw many classroom teachers using the boards as merely very expensive poster hangers and display screens. These teachers did not see the value of this tool, and did not have any voice in choosing it. Therefore, it sat idle without being utilized for its intended purpose.

Too often, districts purchased devices with a one-time funding source, such as a grant. In some instances, minimal Internet connectivity would render the devices all but useless. In others, teachers were unsure why they were receiving these devices or how they were going to use them with their students because no professional development was provided to go along with them. Students are happy to have access to technology, especially if they can do more with it than just type a paper or create a presentation, and administrators are seduced by the idea that providing it will result in gains in student achievement, but those gains can only be realized if a well-conceived plan to effectively incorporate technology is in place.

Blended learning—the integration of anywhere, anytime, Web-based, technology-rich activities and education methods into the existing "brick and mortar" school structure—is difficult to achieve, but is absolutely essential in today's world.

Over the past decade, I have worked closely with classroom teachers and district administrators to incorporate technology into their teaching and learning processes. I have always believed that in order for classroom teachers to use technology as an activator of learning, they need to learn about it in the context of what they are teaching, not as a separate function to be "added in" or saved for Friday funday. Inquiry-oriented lessons or problem-based learning seemed to be the best way to engage teachers and students with learning how to creatively incorporate technology. I also discovered WebQuests, developed by Bernie Dodge, a structure that provides teachers with ways to incorporate problem-based learning with Web 2.0 tools for collaborating, creating, and sharing content online in a safe learning environment.

In addition to thoughtful integration of technology, a shared vision is a strong indicator of success for a transformation to blended learning. It's critical to have all stakeholders value the common direction and embrace the interconnected plans for student success.

I recently partnered with a district where the vision statement appeared on the letterhead, the home page of the district Web site, and on all communications to the staff. Even so, most teachers, parents, and staff could not cite that vision statement when asked to. However, teachers at every grade level, parents, and support staff all knew what the mission of the district was, because every person had embraced the goals they were working toward to support student achievement. Students in this community were expected to go to college. That vision was being upheld through the beliefs and the actions of each member of the learning community, not through the words on the letterhead or home page banner of the district Web site. Eighty-eight percent of graduating students from this district attend college. The culture of achievement was successfully created around the shared vision.

It was through encounters such as these that I began to see the need for a school-wide or district-wide common understanding of the vision for integrating technology into instruction. I became aware that district and site administrators could make more effective decisions if they could see the big picture of their technology adoption and implementation initiatives.

Based on my own experiences and on supporting research, I have found that there are six interrelated arenas within a district that support the evolution of an effective student-centered blended learning environment: Pre-assessment, Leadership and Decision Making, Learning and Development for Teacher Effectiveness, Infrastructure and Facilities, Resources, and Continuous Improvement. Together, I refer to these six arenas as the Framework for Digital Learning Transformation.

There are many paths that a district can travel to a technology-rich blended learning environment. Just as each student has individual learning needs, each district has individual improvement needs and circumstances. This book is designed to provide guidance in utilizing the Framework for Digital Learning Transformation on the journey to blended learning, whatever form that journey might take in your district.

After an overview of blended learning, *The Learning Transformation* focuses on the arenas of the framework. Chapter 1 describes "The Foundations of Blended Learning." Chapter 2, "Shared Leadership and Decision Making," suggests ideas that can help you build a shared vision in your district or school. Chapter 3, "Supporting Teacher Effectiveness for Student Achievement," guides you through the purposeful planning and support necessary to enable academic success among all students in the blended environment.

Chapter 4, "Technology Infrastructure and Facilities," offers insight for leaders surrounding the technical and not-so-technical aspects of the infrastructure required to support student-centered learning goals. This chapter helps the reader understand the bits and bytes and offers recommended strategies and policies related to infrastructure and facilities. Chapter 5, "District Resources," focuses on how resources within the district are utilized and restructured as the move to a blended environment takes shape. There must be a commitment of resources, and it is not only about finding the money to get started, but making sure the financial resources are available and maintained to sustain a technology-rich environment. Personnel, time, content, and devices are the focal points of this chapter.

Chapter 6, "Pre-Assess for Continuous Improvement," focuses on the first and last arenas of the Framework for Digital Learning Transformation. This book ends where your journey will actually begin—with pre-assessment. Plans and decisions must be based on data. One of the biggest mistakes that districts or schools can make is to not take the time to understand their current environment. The data gathered during a pre-assessment of that environment will guide future decisions—*all* of them—for short-, medium-, and long-term goal setting. Based on a strong commitment to support districts in this endeavor, my colleagues and I developed a systemic readiness study called TIPS: Technology Integration Planning Study that is based on the Framework for Digital Learning Transformation and utilizes an evaluative structure centered on a process-based rubric to pre-assess a school's environment and to monitor for continuous improvement.

My colleagues and I hope that the concepts found in this book will help you guide a successful learning transformation in your district.

CHAPTER 1

The Foundations of Blended Learning

The Learning Transformation in Student Environments

The flow of information in the 21st century no longer resembles the learning environments of the relatively recent past. Even so, while the world is now at our fingertips, many students still learn within the four walls of a classroom. Today, there are about 55 million students attending K–12 schools (National Center for Education Statistics, 2014). By the year 2017, an estimated 54 million students will be connected to the Internet (ConnectED, n.d.), and mobile devices will be the most common way that students interact with the Web, both in school and out. Is your district prepared for this shift? According to Education Superhighway (2014), 63 percent of schools nationwide are not ready to implement a 1:1 digital device per child ratio with "bring your own device" policies, due to a lack of bandwidth. And because the rigorous Common Core State Standards require students to be able to research and communicate their ideas using up-to-date technology, the schools that aren't ready for 1:1 implementation aren't ready for the Common Core, either. Schools need to act now to ensure their students are prepared for today's world.

An instructional transformation is needed in our schools. Some teachers, students, and administrators have already begun to see this transformation, but most schools still have far to go in the journey to blended learning. Classrooms need to evolve into a blend of teacher-led instruction and student access to teacher-guided digital content. Teachers must become more and more effective at addressing today's technology-infused world by optimizing student learning environments to support the cognitive complexity of day-to-day academic work. Digital technologies must be utilized in such a way that they help to provide the structure needed to support student-centric, personalized learning environments that are relevant, meaningful, and timely.

Blended learning, or the blending of classroom instruction with customized digital content, is an innovative approach to engaging students and giving them access to the tools and content they need to unlock the unlimited opportunities that now exist for learning anytime and anywhere they have access to the Internet. For teachers, blended learning requires a paradigm shift for preparation and classroom practice. With less emphasis on disseminating information, a teacher's craft must evolve toward facilitating student learning. Meeting both student and teacher needs while designing a curriculum to prepare students for college and career readiness in the digital world is the task of every school leader today.

The variety of blended learning models available for classroom adoption present opportunities for teachers to personalize learning for their students. As districts add hardware, software, and connectivity in schools, the growing accessibility to devices, content, and the Internet creates more equity for students and their learning outcomes. Students who use learning management systems hosted by their schools can work collaboratively and more efficiently. A higher level of student engagement in lessons customizable by digital content and project-based learning can support better student performance.

Blended Learning Models

Blended learning, simply stated, is an innovative approach to education in which students learn in a brick-and-mortar setting but also have access to the tools they need to unlock opportunities to learn anytime and anywhere. Students will do some of their learning with content delivered online while not at school or while not having direct instruction from a teacher.

There are different models for classroom instruction in a blended learning environment. It is important to understand the different models or structures through which blended learning can be delivered, as well as the underlying principles of each model. Teachers may have mastered one or two of these models already, and may be drawn to the model they are most comfortable with. Creating a common definition of blended learning models allows stakeholders in the school to have an understanding of how they can best transform their instruction.

The challenge for a district or site leader is to expose teachers to a wide variety of tools and strategies for their instruction so they may then choose which blended model provides the best learning outcome in their classrooms. Teachers with the ability to utilize all the blended learning models will have the most flexibility to choose the right one for the learning task.

Blended learning can look very different from school to school depending on several factors such as the resources available, the training available to teachers, and student age. However, the primary factor in developing a blended learning program is the academic goals of the school.

Michael Horn and Heather Staker have outlined six of the most common models of blended learning (Horn and Staker, 2011). It is possible to practice several models within an individual school. Think of these different models of blended learning as a continuum moving from teacher-directed, textbook-enhanced teaching and learning to online, student-centric learning (see Figure 1.1).

The **classroom model**, or "face-to-face driver," is the most basic model of blended learning and is dependent upon the teacher delivering most of the instruction, driving the content and pacing according to what the students must learn and what the teacher may know.

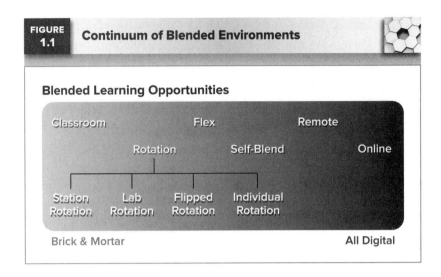

FIGURE 1.1 Continuum of Blended Environments

Blended Learning Opportunities

Classroom   Flex   Remote

Rotation   Self-Blend   Online

Station | Lab | Flipped | Individual
Rotation | Rotation | Rotation | Rotation

Brick & Mortar   All Digital

Students use computers in a computer lab setting or in the classroom if there is a bank of computers available.

The classroom model is a great fit for:

- Schools or districts transitioning from traditional to blended learning environments
- Enrichment and Response to Intervention environments
- Supplemental instruction for English language learners
- Self-paced learning

The **rotation model** is used within a course or class period in which students move between online and classroom instruction. There are four types of the rotation model.

- Station rotation: Within a course or class period, students rotate between different learning modalities, including online learning. Other modalities may include small-group or whole-class instruction, pencil-and-paper assignments, group projects, and individual tutoring

- Lab rotation: Students rotate to a different location within the school building to engage in online learning.
- Flipped classroom: Students rotate between online delivery of content that would typically be delivered by the teacher in the brick-and-mortar classroom outside the school, and classroom time, during which students work through advanced concepts, solve problems, and engage in collaborative learning.
- Individual rotation. Students rotate on an individually created fixed schedule. The teacher sets student schedules based on students' individual needs.

The rotation model is a great fit for:

- Schools that have maximized enrollment or have a lack of space—allowing students to complete online requirements remotely creates new enrollment opportunities
- Schools or districts seeking less radical transitions from traditional learning environments to blended learning environments
- Providing both peer interaction and independent practice for students

In the **flex model**, most of the curriculum is delivered through online content or within a learning management system. Teachers provide on-site support on a flexible or adaptive as-needed basis through small-group and individual tutoring sessions. Each student moves at his or her own pace.

The flex model is a great fit for:

- Personalized instruction
- Accommodating multiple learning modalities
- Schools in need of creative staffing combinations utilizing both certified and uncertified personnel

In the **self-blend,** or **a la carte model,** students choose to take one or more courses entirely online with a teacher-of-record to supplement their traditional instruction at their brick-and-mortar school. Most content is delivered in an online platform and students engage with the content in a flexible format. Students are required to attend meetings at schools or drop-in centers so that teachers can monitor progress and provide face-to-face instruction. Students may be required to meet both synchronously and asynchronously in their online platforms.

The self-blend model is a great fit for:

- AP courses and SAT or ACT preparation
- Niche academic content areas (e.g., Latin, theology)
- Administrators who want to provide blended opportunities for students, but whose districts are not ready to transition to any of the previously listed models

The **remote model** has students take all courses online yet share their time between the brick-and-mortar school site and their remote learning location. They use an online delivery of the content and the instruction. As with the self-blend model, students are required to attend meetings at schools or drop-in centers so that teachers can monitor progress and provide face-to-face instruction. Students may be required to meet both synchronously and asynchronously in their online platforms.

The remote model is a great fit for:

- Students in need of flexible work schedules
- Full-time virtual schools that wish to provide in-person extracurricular opportunities for students
- Students physically unable to attend school on a daily basis
- Mastery-based programs

In the **online lab model,** instruction is delivered through a digital learning platform where students are gathered in a brick-and-mortar lab setting. Instruction is delivered by an online teacher certified in both the subject-area content and the grade level. The lab is supervised by a paraprofessional.

The online lab model is a great fit for:

- Schools that wish to expand their course catalog and don't have trained teachers in specific content areas
- Providing courses with smaller enrollment numbers
- Maximizing financial resources
- Offering multiple courses to multiple students, simultaneously, and in the same space

The **online model** involves courses or classes being delivered online only; students do not come to a brick-and-mortar setting.

The online model is a great fit for:

- Schools that want to expand their course catalog or don't have trained teachers in specific content areas
- Schools that want to offer courses to students of various needs, with educational restraints and/or time restraints

Classroom Schedule and Instruction Models in a Blended Learning Environment

A shift to a blended learning environment changes the time and place students are learning from the traditional set time in a classroom to a flexible time, space, and pace for their learning. Blended learning offers the proponents of both block scheduling and traditional scheduling the opportunity to compromise and develop a new scheduling model that both integrates technology into classrooms and is grounded in best practices designed to maximize student achievement. This scheduling model is appropriate for all K–12 students, rather than a particular grade-specific segment of the learning population. Classrooms designed by the Blended Learning for Alliance School Transformation (BLAST), for example, have created middle school and high school learning environments that have students rotate among two or three learning stations during a two-hour block schedule. The stations involve teacher-led small-group instruction, individualized online learning, and collaborative learning (Walne, 2012). Ninety-minute to two-hour blocks of time have been successfully utilized by many K–5 schools for both reading and mathematics instruction.

A blended learning environment also gives teachers the ability to expand or enhance their current practice of instruction through differentiation, individualization, or personalization of both teaching style and content. The terms *personalization, differentiation,* and *individualization* have different meanings, yet are sometimes used interchangeably. An understanding of what these approaches to instruction are will help bring clarity to how they can be used in a blended learning environment. Differentiation refers to instruction that is *tailored* to the learning *preferences* of different learners. Learning goals are the same for all students, but the method or approach of instruction varies according to the preferences of each student or what research has found works best for students like them. Individualization refers to instruction that is *paced* to the learning *needs* of different learners. Learning goals are the same for all students, but the approach or method of instruction varies according to the preferences of each student, or what research has found works best for students like them. Personalization refers to instruction that is paced to learning needs, tailored to learning preferences, *and* tailored to the specific interests of different learners. In an environment that is fully personalized, the learning objectives and content as well as the method and pace may all vary. Personalization encompasses both differentiation and individualization (U.S. Department of Education, n.d.).

FIGURE 1.2 The Framework for Digital Learning Transformation

The Framework for Digital Learning Transformation

In an environment of systems and structures, it is helpful to understand where variables within a system fit, how they support each other, and how to relate to the whole. The Framework for Digital Learning Transformation provides a structure to visualize relationships among six different arenas needed in digitally rich, blended learning environments (see Figure 1.2). This framework has been developed through partnerships with schools and districts integrating technology into their learning environments and has been shaped by research, anecdotal observations and interviews, and the case studies of early adopters. The framework provides a clear image of the interconnectedness of all parts of the system that influence a blended learning environment. The six arenas are: Pre-assessment, Leadership and Decision Making, Learning and Development for Teacher Effectiveness, Infrastructure and Facilities, Resources, and Continuous Improvement (Figure 1.3).

Use the Framework for Digital Learning Transformation as a guide for the governance and implementation of blended learning models. Clearly planned goals for implementing a blended learning environment and the subsequent monitoring of the implementation will result in a successful learning transformation centered on student achievement.

Pre-Assessment

Planning for a digitally rich blended learning environment begins with an understanding of the school or district's current learning environment. A pre-assessment can provide the data needed to create short-, medium- and long-term goals as well as the action planning steps needed to achieve those goals.

A thoughtful pre-assessment can troubleshoot potential issues before they arise and can have an impact on teacher and student success. Readiness to implement new initiatives for blended learning environments will take the representation of all stakeholders on a leadership team to reinvent a vision for the mission. A pre-assessment allows you to identify what impacts teaching, learning, productivity, and policies within the context of the five remaining arenas of learning transformation: Leadership and Decision Making, Learning and Development for Teacher Effectiveness, Infrastructure and Facilities, Resources, and Continuous Improvement.

FIGURE 1.3 **Arenas of the Framework for Digital Learning Transformation**

Pre-Assessment

Identify systemic and organizational performance indicators that impact teaching, learning, policies, and productivity in the district. Conducting a pre-assessment of the five remaining arenas is a way to determine the current status of the educational landscape in the district or at the school site. Gathering baseline data in these arenas is critical for determining the strategy for integrating technology into the learning system.

Leadership and Decision Making

The capacity of the school/district, through leadership (e.g., superintendent, principals, board members, and building-level teams), to operate from a shared vision of technology that is characterized by the belief that a comprehensive, integrated approach to technology-enriched teaching and learning will improve student performance. This includes a clear decision-making process, agreed-upon roles for key stakeholders, and the commitment of resources to support the transformation throughout the district.

Learning and Development for Teacher Effectiveness

The degree to which teachers are prepared and supported in their efforts to facilitate and inspire student learning and creativity and to design and develop digital-age learning experiences and assessments for student-centered instruction and full integration of technology.

Infrastructure and Facilities

The capacity of the school/district to build and maintain a reliable, flexible, and high-quality technological infrastructure in which there is appropriate information security and which is easily available (e.g., user-friendly) to all students and staff whenever and wherever needed. This includes: technical support; hardware, software, and communication components; ready access to networked resources (e.g., LAN, WAN, and Web); and assistive technology for special needs students.

Resources

The degree to which the district supports educational goals through the identification and provision of educational content, and through ensuring that fiscal and human resources are in place to support strategic goals and educational outcomes.

Continuous Improvement

The capacity of the district and school to systematically provide reliable assessments in order to determine the strengths and areas that need improvement for all staff and students. The data provided from these assessments should be accurate and available in real time. A process should be in place to use the information obtained to develop or change current practices in order to improve student learning.

When conducting pre-assessments, areas of knowledge can fall into three categories. The first two categories—the things you *know* you know, and the things you know you *don't* know—can be completely and adequately addressed through self-assessment. The challenge for many districts venturing into the digital learning space is that there are things leaders *don't* know they don't know. The value of both internal and external pre-assessments is to identify what we *don't* know we don't know. Implementing sustainable improvements in a learning environment requires determining the needs and capabilities of a school by evaluating such things as teacher readiness, available bandwidth, IT support tools, district or community resources, and contingency plans. For example, if a school decides to procure new tablet devices for a 1:1 initiative (one device for each student), how well can the IT department sustain the technology over the course of the next two years after their introduction into the school? If leadership is focusing on the immediacy and excitement of the implementation, the question of sustainability may fall into the "I don't know I don't know" category. With data in hand from a thoughtful pre-assessment, the planning for informed short-, medium- and long-term goals can begin.

Leadership and Decision Making

A successful digital learning transformation will require the collective vision of all school leaders to accomplish the goal of promoting student achievement in the new blended classroom environment. It is an exciting time for learning transformation in education, and it is exciting to be an agent of that change. Collaborative leadership is the right approach to guide integrated technology-enriched teaching and learning. Consider what students, teachers, administrators, and community members value, and engage them in clear and open communication to understand how each member will best work with the others. As they move into a more student-centric learning environment that includes the use of technology, districts will need to begin re-evaluating their culture to identify (Stein, 1998; Lambert, 1998; Fullan, 2001; DuFour and Eaker, 1998; Hord, 1998):

- A widely shared sense of purpose and values
- Norms of continuous improvement
- A commitment to and sense of responsibility for the learning of all students
- Collaborative, communicative, and collegial relationships
- Opportunities for staff reflection, collective inquiry, and sharing personal practice and successes

Advancing a vision for a successful blended environment—with students engaged in the curriculum and teachers prepared to integrate technology into the core curriculum—requires collaborative planning, including clear decision-making processes, defined roles for stakeholders, and the planned commitment of resources.

Priorities to focus on during this planning stage include a comprehensive financial plan, dedicated resources, allocations for infrastructure improvements, allowances for upgrades and maintenance, a multi-year district budget analysis, and permanent line items built in to ensure support of digital learning transformation. Finally, a plan for implementation that is consistently measured and monitored is key to ongoing success.

Leaders bring about a new or re-imagined culture to a school or district by changing the educational practices there and injecting them with new ideas. The idea of "reculturing" stems from the work of Fullan (2001), which describes the positive shift in thinking required for the change from a teacher-centric culture to a student-centric culture. Districts need to reculture, not reorganize or start over, by cultivating open innovation among faculty. Reculturing allows teachers to integrate new knowledge into their work and create new ways to more effectively practice their craft (Randolph, 2009). Leading the reculturing of a district through the lens of adding technological tools and digital assets to activate student-centered blended learning requires leaders to:

- Clarify a vision and define the shared vision
- Identify key questions for the district and possible solutions
- Evaluate teacher readiness and feasible professional development for teacher effectiveness
- Evaluate on-site personnel
- Solidify technology infrastructure and learning management system platforms early in the blended learning initiative
- Focus on implementation, not procurement; think it through, including teacher training and tech support
- Insist on quality content

Learning and Development for Teacher Effectiveness

Professional development for teachers in a digital learning environment can sometimes be overwhelming. There is an almost unlimited amount of readily available content to choose from. What makes a classroom blended learning environment successful is how teachers build their daily practice of making digital content usable to students while addressing the standards they need to teach. Teachers will benefit from professional development experiences that prepare them to use blended learning models creatively and strategically with their students to add meaning to the digital content and tools they use.

Infrastructure and Facilities

A robust technological infrastructure is necessary to support blended learning. For technology to be ubiquitous and give universal access to students and teachers alike, a reliable network must be in place, with facilities and structures designed to meet student needs in a connected and collaborative classroom. Planning for infrastructure includes designing interoperable systems that smooth information transfer, building network capacity that can handle the added demand, and nurturing human resources that can support the delivery of digital content to students and teachers. Some big-picture considerations that bring value include hosting a learning management system at schools so that all digital content is accessible in one place. The design of facilities and structures will need to change to meet student needs for an Internet connected, collaborative classroom.

Resources

As technology gaps become evident in classroom environments, school and district leaders are mobilizing district resources to optimize achievement for their students. Although putting technology in our schools may seem as easy as buying the tools for faculty to use with their increasingly technology-savvy students, moving into a blended learning environment without a clear plan can result in lackluster outcomes. The purposeful implementation of technology and digital content in the new classroom paradigm is much more important than the procurement of the tools students and teachers use. Schools that plan carefully the task of balancing the explosive potential technology holds with the higher priority of helping teachers teach and students learn will find their time and resources well spent.

The capacity of the district to support a technology-rich student-centered learning environment with finances, personnel, and instructional content is dependent upon a solid plan for resources and a thoughtful infrastructure to support educational goals.

Continuous Improvement

Evidence from across the country continues to show that the increased use of technology in a blended learning environment is improving student and teacher productivity. Districts are reporting reading, math, and science gains with students in all ethnic and socioeconomic groups since expanding the use of technology. Some districts report that blended learning is reducing the dropout rate and that students are more likely to earn a high school diploma as a result of access to online courses (Staker, 2011). Many districts are utilizing 1:1 laptop programs to improve student learning. The schools that have achieved the best results have benefitted from the deliberate implementation and monitoring of a cycle of continuous improvement. Revisiting and refining strategic goals and monitoring the success of implementations using ongoing, reliable data to inform the decision-making process creates a cycle of continuous improvement. Monitoring improvement and sharing the results allows the cultivation of a school culture that creates and demonstrates collaborative and shared responsibility for the success of each student.

The Transition to Blended Learning

The Framework for Digital Learning Transformation provides school leaders with a roadmap to navigate the shift from a traditional learning environment to a blended learning environment. It provides a structure that enables leaders to see the interconnectedness of the key decision-making arenas in the transition to a blended learning environment. The six arenas are intertwined and support cohesive leadership actions. There is not one arena that has a greater value than another; rather, each is designed to work in concert to support the development of a blended environment for student-centered individualized learning.

Innovation begins with leadership. Leadership begins with innovation. District and site leaders create conditions for success in the transformation from a traditional classroom model to a digitally rich blended learning environment through engaged leadership to ensure stakeholders within the district become involved and embrace the new student-centered paradigm we call blended learning.

CHAPTER 2

Shared Leadership and Decision Making

Imagine a district with a 100 percent graduation rate, where students are motivated to learn and are engaged on a metacognitive level because they are curious and have opportunities to choose what they learn. With access to information any place they go, at any time of the day or evening, they are connecting with their peers from their classes and with other students and scholars all over the globe. Innovative thinking is embraced by their teachers and expected of them.

Imagine a school where everyone knows the shared vision for transformative learning environments and supports the vision and the purpose and the mission of the school. The teachers are purposeful in what they are teaching and are able to focus on the process of learning rather than only the end result. Regular and immediate feedback is available to students during their learning progress, so that learning can happen not only as a result of what the teacher does, but also as a result of what the *student* does. Collaboration among school leaders occurs both vertically and horizontally and across grade levels. Principals use social media outlets to connect with parents and students to provide immediate access to information about events at school. Everyone believes they are making a difference in the lives of the students, as is evidenced by universal access to the data available for decision making in the classroom, the school, and the district.

If this is the culture that you would like to see in your school, you are probably wondering what conditions are necessary to cultivate this type of environment. There are many paths a school or district

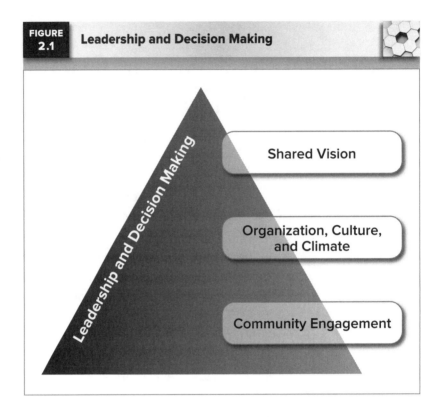

FIGURE 2.1 Leadership and Decision Making

can take to develop a culture that will support the innovation that is needed to transition to a blended learning environment.

The arena of Leadership and Decision Making within the Framework for Digital Learning Transformation (Figure 2.1) is designed to help leaders in the early planning phases develop a unique, district- or school-wide shared vision to establish the foundation for future change. The key component of a shared vision is the belief that a comprehensive, integrated approach to blended learning will improve student performance. The steps outlined here will orient leaders to the task of cultivating a shared vision among principals, board members, and building-level teams to integrate blended learning into the school environment.

Also included in this arena of the Framework for Digital Learning Transformation are processes for establishing clear decision-making practices for stakeholders as well as identifying the roles of key stakeholders. Roles include accessing student and community input, developing strategic goals, designing guiding questions to direct future actions, carrying out those actions, and managing the steps toward implementation of a blended learning environment.

Qualities of a Blended Learning Leader

Leaders who have successfully led district-wide technology integration initiatives and district-wide teaching and learning transformations exhibit notable qualities, the most important of which is the core belief that *all* students can learn and succeed. Successful leaders have a commitment to students and to learning. They nurture an environment that embraces collaboration and shared leadership, and they do not dispute the validity of failure. They espouse a growth mindset and they model the actions and expectations they are asking others to commit to. For example, if you, as the district or site leader, are asking your staff to utilize a collaborative site for communication and sharing, then you should use the site for your communication with them. Modeling behaviors or expectations in a new learning environment supports the staff growth that is desired. As a leader, you should show through your actions the commitment and dedication you have to this transformation. Lead by example.

The strength of your belief in the initiative will sustain you to overcome obstacles as you build and support a blended learning model that will give every student the opportunity to have personalized and individualized learning experiences. Understanding your own strengths and the areas in which you need to grow will help you respond to any challenges that might be ahead. Like an entrepreneur, you must take your idea and hold it dear. Initial failures often lead to future successes.

Successful leaders of digital learning transformations possess many of the following qualities:

- **Visionary leaders** hold onto an idea of what the future of teaching and learning could be and enlist others to design new models and approaches that will help transform that vision into reality.

- **Flexible leaders** balance planning with intelligent flexibility to allow each failure or snag to be a learning experience. They adapt to situations and are open to receiving feedback, using it to develop their skills and learn from their mistakes.

- **Communicative leaders** share thoughts with all stakeholders through both conversation and personal action. They listen and act on the voices of others.

- **Courageous leaders** have the ability to stand alone and to support others as they meet with challenges. They foster supportive, shared leadership and relinquish the idea that they are in control.

- **Resilient leaders** have long vision and are relentlessly focused on it. They have the ability to bounce back from setbacks, to learn from failures, and to be motivated by challenges that will bring their vision to life.

- **Reflective leaders** think deeply about personal and systemic actions and the intended outcome of those actions. They embrace feedback from others to complement their own personal reflection and gain a deeper understanding about what is going well, what should be modified, and what can be eliminated.

- **Gritty leaders** have a passion and a deep-down, bone-rattling belief in the long-term goal. They have the ability to overcome obstacles and challenges that stand in the way of achieving long-term goals, and will never give up. They will do whatever it takes to get the job done.

You may recognize several of these qualities in yourself, and will likely also know which of these you don't fully embrace. Think about a few of the aforementioned qualities that may not be as representative of you, and concentrate on developing them. As you develop a better sense of positive leadership qualities, you may find that your days don't seem quite so long, and the nights not so short. Preparing students to be productive citizens in a digital society and successful in a world that is rapidly evolving is a challenge, and will require resilience and determination.

From Mission to Shared Vision

Schools are preparing a generation of students for the challenges of a globalized world, and digital tools are accelerating the process of change in schools and districts. To meet the needs of students in today's ever-changing society, leadership should have a clear sense of the academic goals of the district or school and be prepared to communicate the mission of the school in a cohesive, condensed way. If a parent at a school function inquires about the direction the school or district is heading, the answer to this question, related with brevity, is the mission of the school or district. Understanding and owning the mission of the school will serve to drive the passion needed in communications to stakeholders as you transition to a blended learning environment.

Once you understand your district's mission, you should clarify your personal view of what you *hope* can be possible for your school or district. Defining the nexus between your personal vision, the district's mission, the hopes of the teachers and parents, and the future needs of the students is paramount in leading a digital learning transformation. Understanding your own personal vision gives you the courage to work collaboratively with colleagues and other stakeholders as you forge a plan in uncharted territory that defines the future of learning. Your vision will be the driver behind your actions while you implement a blended learning environment.

Your school or district most likely already has a mission statement. Take it out and read over it a few times. Does it represent the vision you have just created in your mind? Think of the school or district you would want to create if there were no limitations in budgets, time, or staffing (see Figure 2.2). What would the school environment look, sound, and feel like? What would leaders, teachers, and students be doing? What would students be learning that will prepare them for college and careers? How are support staff involved? Are administrators communicating with and supporting teachers and students? Is innovation a key ingredient? Then, ask yourself what the pedagogical

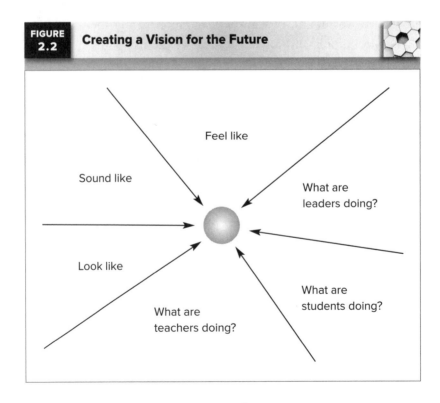

FIGURE 2.2   Creating a Vision for the Future

Feel like

Sound like

What are leaders doing?

Look like

What are teachers doing?

What are students doing?

differences are between what you see in your vision and what you see in your organization today.

Through regular and clear communication on the progress of the goals for any initiative implementation, and by involving the community of stakeholders in the decision-making process, you will nurture a culture of inclusive, creative learning. First and foremost, remember you are leading a change for students, where technology creates the opportunity for a more personalized, deeper learning experience.

Transforming a school into a blended environment takes the shared vision of all stakeholders—the collective belief that will build and sustain the blended learning environment. Top-down initiatives rarely result in successful systemic change (Lucey, 2008). An initiative such as transforming student learning environments into models of blended learning cannot be handed down, nor will it build from a groundswell of well-intentioned practitioners. Invite representatives from different parts of the school or district, including members of the IT department, to take part in the development of the vision. This collaboration creates a culture of shared ownership of the vision and has a better chance at succeeding. A well-articulated vision will unite stakeholders for a greater purpose.

Student success depends upon beginning the process of creating a shared vision with defining the academic goals that will guide every decision made. To prevent an unnecessary roller-coaster ride where the purchase and use of devices might trump the development and implementation of instructional strategies, keep the shared vision clearly communicated and in front of you as you make decisions about expenditures.

Many districts have introduced technology devices into classrooms because it seemed like the right thing to do. In the rush to put technology in classrooms, the goals for optimal educational outcomes that were to be achieved with the help of these device-driven initiatives often were not articulated. The proliferation and subsequent misuse of interactive whiteboards is a prime example. District and site leaders had the desire to add devices to enhance learning, but the lack of a shared vision for what an interactive classroom might look like and how this device might help students learn prevented the best outcome in many classrooms.

Decision-Making Teamwork

Leading a learning transformation is collaborative in nature and characterized by the belief that a comprehensive, integrated approach to technology-rich teaching and learning will improve student performance. Transforming a school culture into a blended learning environment requires a multitude of perspectives to initiate and sustain change. Empowering others to share in the decision-making process by allowing them to make decisions transforms leadership into a shared responsibility. Leaders have the opportunity to cultivate a shared vision at the beginning of the planning stages that includes nurturing a desire for innovation among team members.

The essential work of a transformational leader is to provide an environment where creativity and inspiration are encouraged and embraced. While not all members of the community might be ready to jump right in, allowing them time to see the enthusiasm build and the successes grow will enable reluctant community members to begin to embrace the vision. No single individual has the knowledge or decision-making authority to produce sustainable change, but all stakeholders working together can get the job done. Everyone touched by a learning transformation should have an opportunity to be involved. Successful leaders can quell thoughts of fear and uncertainty in their school cultures and instead cultivate thoughts of certainty and ownership for new initiatives. By inviting everyone to participate in a shared decision-making process, the shift that needs to happen in pedagogy and in the culture becomes driven by those who are making the changes. A community that cultivates innovation, openly shares, and helps one another feels the most ownership in any change initiative. Even if every individual is not able to be directly involved in decision-making processes, representation from their group will make them more likely to embrace and value the outcomes of decision making. Create a collaborative team with representatives from all constituencies—students, teachers, parents, school board members, and donors—to plan the transformation of the learning environment.

Establishing an innovations team or management team to plan for the transformation of the current school culture and to ensure pervasive communication about those plans brings guidance to the overall process. Continuous communication through e-mail, online user groups, wikis, or other collaborative documents supports a collaborative environment and gives voice to all stakeholders. In order to give full recognition to this team, develop a calendar and set dates for meeting times. Emphasize the importance of this valuable team by setting future meeting dates before meetings begin. From the initial planning stages to the full implementation of a blended learning environment, monitoring progress and sharing information with all constituents in a timely and regular manner is critical to success.

A broad representation of stakeholders on the innovations team brings a wider perspective to the process and a greater range of expertise to fill the different roles and responsibilities of the team. Including district-level administrators establishes accountability and brings a systemic view to the team. Administrators can share with team members the district objectives as well as state and federal guidelines, ensuring a big-picture perspective. Principals and assistant principals bring their perspectives from different levels within the district and will be the strongest catalyst at the building level to lead a cultural and instructional shift. Include a range of teachers from different grade levels, content areas, and specialties, including paraprofessionals and other non-teaching staff. This group will become teacher leaders. Parents appreciate opportunities to participate in school decisions as well, and student representatives can be the most valuable assets to the decision-making process. School board members can assist in areas where board approval for funding is needed. A representative from the teacher's union leadership opens communication lines early on for a deeper understanding of the learning transformation they

FIGURE 2.3 | **Checklist of Innovations Team Members**

☐ School district's cabinet and central office administrators

☐ Principals

☐ Technology director (and IT department representatives)

☐ Research and evaluation department members

☐ Civic leaders, Chamber of Commerce members, business leaders, industry partners

☐ Higher education and trade school representatives

☐ Teacher's union leaders

☐ School board members

☐ Teachers

☐ Students

☐ Parents

FIGURE 2.4 | **First Responsibilities of the Innovations Team**

• Establish guiding questions that will help target the key objectives

• Develop SMARTER strategic goal statements

• Develop common definitions of words that could be misconstrued or misinterpreted

• Develop a plan of action

• Decide how to measure results and use data to inform decisions

• Design a management plan for implementation

will contribute to. Civic leaders and local business leaders in the community have a vested interest in the schools, and cultivating their support is invaluable. Data experts or representatives from the research and assessment department will bring an important expertise to inform and support the success of the implementation. Figure 2.3 shows a list of people to include on the innovations team.

Once the members of the innovations team are chosen, they can begin the work of planning for the transformation to blended learning. Figure 2.4 outlines the innovations team's initial responsibilities.

Establish Guiding Questions

An initial activity for the innovations team could be to investigate and evaluate the six arenas of the Framework for Digital Learning Transformation and begin to brainstorm questions about each (see Figure 2.5). Guiding questions uncover prevalent assumptions and help lead the next task of developing strategic goal statements. Guiding questions can also assist in making sure needs are identified and met as plans are developing.

FIGURE 2.5 **Sample Guiding Questions**

Framework Arena	Guiding Questions
Pre-Assessment	
The pre-assessment will address the guiding questions from all framework arenas	• What is the current learning landscape of the district? • How does technology support the current learning landscape?
Leadership and Decision Making	
Shared vision	• How is the vision developed within the district? • How does inquiry play a role in the visioning process?
Organization, culture, climate	• How is the vision collaborative among all stakeholders? • What are the goals of the district? • Does the district's current environment provide students with the opportunity to learn the skills necessary for college or careers?
Community engagement	• Who are the stakeholders and how are they involved?
Learning and Development for Teacher Effectiveness	
Student-centered learning	• What opportunities are available for students to explore their own interests? • How prepared are teachers to leverage technology and digital tools to enhance instruction and learning? • How prepared are administrators to lead this effort?
Professional growth	• What opportunities are available for faculty to stay current in technology, instruction, and curriculum?
Curriculum design	• What is the observable evidence that students use technologies to engage in inquiry processes, sustain curiosity, create content, and creatively express their learning?

FIGURE 2.5 **Sample Guiding Questions** (continued)

Framework Arena	Guiding Questions
Infrastructure and Facilities	
Facilities Facilities and schedules maximize the learning opportunities that technology enables	• How are schedules, facilities, and classrooms dynamically arranged to support the learning needs of students using technology?
Information technology IT staff support innovation in teaching and learning	• In what ways do IT staff and their systems support the leaning innovations of faculty and students as they integrate technology in the learning environment?
Resources	
Personnel	• How are personnel utilized to meet the demands of a technology-infused environment?
Financial	• How are district technology initiatives funded?
Instructional content Curriculum design is rigorous and innovative to leverage technology	• What is the observable evidence that students use technologies to engage in inquiry processes, sustain curiosity, create content, and creatively express their learning?
Continuous Improvement	
Progress monitoring	• How do the data collected and analyzed over time inform the progress, success, and sustainability of the vision and goals of the district? • What is the relationship between the district's strategic goals and the move to a digitally rich learning environment? • How does qualitative evidence, such as teacher and student attitudes toward learning and community support, inform the progress, success, and sustainability of the vision and goals of the district?

Develop Strategic Goal Statements— SMARTER Goals

Goal statements are specific statements that identify what needs to be accomplished throughout the process of transforming learning environments while supporting the vision and mission of the district or school. Begin developing strategic goal statements by revisiting goals that are currently in place to determine if they need to be revised, removed, or created anew. Create goal statements for each of the six arenas of the Framework for Digital Learning Transformation to ensure you do not focus on only one or two areas.

SMART goals have five elements to them. Goals that are SMART are: **S**—strategic, have a **M**—measurable outcome, are **A**—achievable or attainable with the resources available to make them happen, **R**—relevant, and are **T**—time-bound, with a clear time frame to the work. To make them SMARTER, you must: **E**—embark on the journey! (if you never get started on developing goal statements, your goals will never be met) and **R**—reflect, revisit, and revise. Your goals may need mid-course adjustments. The data you gather will help inform you of the need to revise your goals.

A mid-sized district had a desire to create a student-centered blended learning environment. They began by initiating the use of a learning management system to house instructional content. They were gearing up for the integration of a 1:1 student-to-device ratio and needed to upgrade their infrastructure in a timely manner to support the learning goals of the district. A professional development plan was needed to support the classroom teachers and building principals with scaffolded, ongoing support. The district seemed to be a well-oiled machine with a good plan in place supported with goals. Their goals, however, were built around the education system of the past century and had a lack of measurable variables.

When they evaluated their goals, they discovered a need to re-create goals that were SMARTER by revising or adjusting them to align with a student-centered, digitally rich environment. Collectively, they created action steps to achieve the goals that had been sitting idle. They are now in the process of working toward integrating laptops a grade level at a time, while a learning management system is being introduced and a digitally rich, rigorous curriculum is being developed.

Revisiting goals to make them more relevant to blended learning initiatives is a great way to use the power of an innovations team.

Develop Common Definitions

There are many defined models of blended learning. Six have been shared in the first chapter. These six models are a good place to start, but there is continuous progress being made with digital content to integrate analytic capabilities for greater personalization. The next generation of content may lead to the potential for an even more personalized blended learning model. Students will have multiple opportunities to interact with text and multimedia, and to engage in peer collaboration within a screen of content. Engage faculty across all disciplines, grades, and campuses in thoughtful discussions around the skills they believe students need to be successful today and to thrive in the future. Create the blended learning models that meet the needs of your students, and then create a common language about those models to use in your school or district. A glossary of terms useful in developing common definitions is included in this volume. Creating new or understanding existing definitions is a step to building a community of collaboration.

The leadership team of Exeter Unified School District in the Central Valley of California was preparing to create a blended learning environment. After researching the different models of blended learning, they had a better understanding of its complexities, such as the expectation for students to gain control over their learning, and for teachers to support the individualization of learning goals for students. Leaders participated in an activity in which each thought of words and phrases that represented what blended learning meant to them. They winnowed down their ideas to best represent the commonalities. Some phrases they narrowed to included *student learning, multiple modes of instruction, balance of tools, structures, engagement, global citizens, problem-based learning, application-based learning,* and *unlimited learning settings.* They then integrated these ideas into their definition of blended learning: "The highest level of student learning occurs with multiple modes of instruction using a balance of tools and structures that provides engagement through application-based learning in unlimited learning settings."

With this group-created definition, Exeter USD now "owns" a concept of blended learning and has a common understanding of the direction they will pursue.

Develop a Plan of Action

Districts will have strategic plans. School sites will have their school improvement plans or strategic goals. Revisit these plans and make sure that the goals developed by the innovations team are reflected in the current plans. It is important to develop blended learning action steps within the strategic or school improvement plans that determine very specifically *what* needs to be accomplished, *when* the action/activity will need to be completed, what resources will be needed, who is responsible for seeing it through, and how its success will be measured. Build in time for reflection about each of the strategic goals to evaluate them for mid-course adjustments. Figure 2.6 outlines the elements of a successful implementation strategy.

FIGURE 2.6	Elements of a Successful Implementation Strategy	

- A clear, transparent decision-making process
- Agreed-upon roles for key stakeholders
- A plan for the commitment of resources
- A plan for continuous improvement to ensure successful implementation

Preparing to move to a blended learning environment, a small district had performed a pre-assessment of each of the arenas of the Framework for Digital Learning Transformation. In the arena of Leadership and Decision Making, several action components were found to be missing from the district's strategic plan. The team discovered they needed to update instructional materials so that they could be delivered in a digital format. The equipment students needed to use and the content also needed updating.

The leadership team has since created new SMART goals and outlined the action steps needed to find quality digital math content and the technical equipment to support its use in the classroom.

To facilitate communication within the community, host a kick-off open house to create awareness and build on the newly articulated vision with parents and community members. This first meeting will provide a time to discuss the concept of blended learning and the role technology plays in enhancing student learning. This first meeting is also a time to listen to community members and their input. A second open house can be scheduled to explain goals, timelines, and budgets. The SMARTER goals created or revised by the innovations team could also be shared at a community meeting. To sustain community support, hold quarterly information-sharing events that include all stakeholders and address the progress of the implementation. Feedback from the community is as important as sharing updates on progress made. Plan to share information and receive feedback through online surveys and telephone or text polls, and have a plan to incorporate feedback effectively. Successes can be celebrated at these events. Even the smallest success is worthy of celebration.

Use Data to Inform Decisions

Decisions should be made with reference to data. The data collected during a pre-assessment of the district or school site and the learning environment can be used for guiding short-term, medium-term, and long-term goals. (See Chapter 6 for a detailed look at pre-assessment.) Once SMART goals are established, determine a plan of action, and create measurable benchmarks along the way.

Project Management

The transition to a blended learning environment has many moving parts. Teams will be meeting on a regular basis. Contracted vendors, professional development providers, and hardware and software personnel will be involved in many aspects of the transition. Teacher leaders and district administrators wear numerous hats already, and while there may be a variety of committee chairs, or district champions for the various parts of the initiative, assigning a single person to manage or coordinate all aspects of the outside influences will keep things moving forward.

Commitment to a successful transition requires supporting the change of teacher practices and student behaviors. A dedicated project manager can oversee the logistics of the implementation process. Project managers might oversee the following processes for blended learning implementation:

- Procurement
- Networking requirements
- Contracts with external vendors and consultants (district based or site based)
- Technology infrastructure
- Devices
- Online content
- Data integration
- Funding

Additionally, the design of curriculum and the design of classrooms for the new blended learning paradigm will need support personnel. An outside partner may be required to offer expertise that is not available within the district. Roles and responsibilities should be outlined at the onset between the project manager, district staff, school staff, and any external consultants.

From Vision to Reality

The arena of shared leadership and decision making supports the use of an integrated approach in the transition to a technology-enriched teaching and learning environment. Leaders must strongly believe in the vision of what student-centered learning can be. Possessing a deep understanding of oneself is a prerequisite to the ability to motivate others and sustain high energy through changing times through leading by example and cultivating a shared vision with all stakeholders. Leadership is not driven from the top down. A leader's primary role is to create a culture of collaboration and shared decision making. Establishing teams for community involvement in the development of strategic plans and goals, and creating a project manager role to oversee the logistics of all of the moving parts are among the steps needed to establish the innovative culture required to sustain change.

Once the community is engaged and participating in the decisions necessary to move to a blended environment, the next step is to prepare teachers for the transition in their classrooms. Fear can be an inhibitor for teachers bringing devices into their classrooms. Technology sometimes won't work, or students may know more about the devices and how to use them than their teachers do. It can be intimidating to explore and make the mistakes that will eventually bring about comfort with the new technology. Teachers who have had representation for or direct input into the decisions being made will be ready for the coming changes, and will be more open and less fearful about learning how to incorporate digital tools into teaching and learning.

CHAPTER 3

Supporting Teacher Effectiveness for Student Achievement

Roxanne is entering her first day of seventh grade excited to receive the tablet device that her school will be loaning students for the year. Mark, her teacher, is entering the school building on this first day of school anxiously thinking about the assembly where nearly 300 students will be receiving tablet devices, with some of them making their way to his classroom. Mark has been teaching for nearly 20 years. His students respect him and learn in his classroom. He is nervous, because he thinks the students will know more than he does about the new devices. He is worried the devices will become a distraction to the students and will disrupt the structure he has set up in his class. Although the district provided a two-hour session for teachers on how to use the tablet, with a day of in-service for technology training, Mark has very little idea how to incorporate the new devices effectively to promote student learning. And Mark knows that this year, the tablet will be in Roxanne's backpack more often than not.

This is a scene that has happened in schools over and over again. Devices are purchased, or software installed, without deep support for teachers on the methodology or pedagogy for a student-centered environment. Just as unfortunately, teachers are not able to utilize the devices to their full potential.

Supporting teacher effectiveness is the most important challenge leaders face in positively impacting student learning. Before integrating new technology, we owe it to students and teachers to provide a clear and focused vision of the desired learning outcomes that should take place in a student-centric blended learning environment and then provide them with the tangible professional development opportunities they need to be successful in integrating technology into their classrooms in purposeful ways. Teachers need to be equipped to make informed decisions about how to best serve students in meeting academic standards and developing the skills necessary to learn and thrive in today's global society.

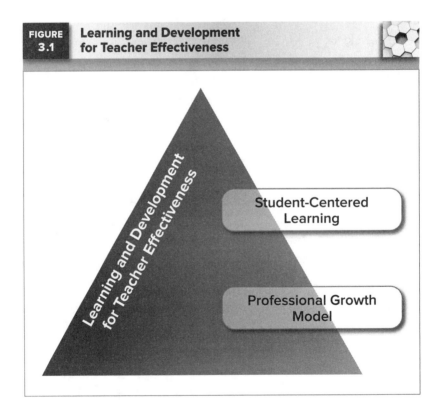

FIGURE 3.1 Learning and Development for Teacher Effectiveness

Learning and Development for Teacher Effectiveness

Student-Centered Learning

Professional Growth Model

The arena of Learning and Development for Teacher Effectiveness within the Framework for Digital Learning Transformation (Figure 3.1) supports the professional growth of teachers with respect to both the integration of technology tools and the support of individualized student learning.

As administrators or classroom teachers, the desired impact of our decisions and actions is to facilitate meaningful learning in a safe environment. In districts across the country, administrators are purchasing technology in anticipation of, or in reaction to, a pedagogical shift to a student-centered digital learning environment. Laptops, learning management systems, tablets, smart boards, and mobile devices are finding their way into schools everywhere. In theory, adding technology to schools is a very good thing. However, imagine for just a moment that we were to inject similar waves of technology into our hospitals on a massive scale, while providing doctors, nurses, and administrative staff with no training on how to properly use them. There would certainly be discontent amongst both patients and hospital staff. Educators have experienced a similar frustration. School leaders must remain mindful that technology should not be the primary outcome of a transition to a digital learning environment; rather, it should be a tool used to support the desired teaching and learning outcomes for the school. Our strategic initiatives must always be linked to content standards and student achievement. Teachers need professional development to support the seamless implementation of technology into their practice in innovative and effective ways.

Designing Professional Development

Professional development opportunities experienced in a blended environment for teachers, administrators, and support personnel provide a good foundation for the acquisition of technical skills and an understanding of how students might learn better with appropriate technology. Through participation in valuable development days, teachers and staff will have opportunities to collaborate on strategies for guiding student use of technology while modeling appropriate learning strategies with the wealth of information available online. Teachers and administrators venturing into the world of blended learning should be able to anticipate and celebrate changes in their own beliefs about what joyful, engaging, and successful learning can look like in a transformational, blended learning environment.

When effective implementation is ensured through appropriate development opportunities for staff, there is an increased likelihood that students will experience engaging, student-centered classrooms equipped with digital tools that support and enhance student learning. But a great deal must happen before devices are purchased and placed in students' and teachers' hands. Access to technology does not ensure academic achievement, nor does it ensure high levels of student engagement. Professional development plans should align with the strategic goals of the district. As we develop plans for interactive blended environments, we must be purposeful and develop initiatives with student achievement at the center of all that we do.

Individualized student learning is student centered. In addition to understanding any new technology, teachers will need to know, understand, and incorporate a wide variety of instructional methodologies as well as content in their teaching. An administrator's primary obligation is to create a sense of focus so that teachers have a clear understanding of the blended learning models that exist, and what blended learning can look, sound, and feel like with the technology they have available. The position of teachers in the academic universe is changing. Successful blended environments don't require the teacher to be the focal point of the classroom and can often be more effective when teachers are *not* the focus of instruction. In a blended learning model, the teacher becomes a facilitator and guide, while also providing the knowledge and insight into the course material that they always have. Teachers will be coaches as well as being sources of knowledge and skill. A successful transition to an effective blended model is one in which educators know, based on student needs, when and how to use their various roles as teachers, guides, and facilitators.

If we compare the traditional classroom model to our solar system, the sun around which all things revolve is the teacher. While we may want to say the student is at the center, if we look honestly at our traditional education models, it is teachers, not students, who are front and center in the academic solar system. Teachers, not students, exert the most energy in the classroom. Teachers still view themselves as the primary source of academic light. The prevailing thought is that without the teacher's wisdom shining as the central focus of our classrooms, our students, much like earth's organisms without the sun, will not grow. This is a model that has been accepted and replicated for generations, and with good cause. For centuries educators have been our most valuable sources of knowledge, information, and insight. Now, in the digital age, students increasingly won't see teachers as heliocentric in the classroom solar system. They are now used to finding information themselves or figuring out how to research and do things on their own. Not only does the digital learning transformation create a shift in teaching and learning, but it also shifts the delivery style of professional development. The administrator's role in a blended model is to provide tools and training for teachers in order to bolster this new type of learner.

Innovation takes time. To make lasting changes to a learning culture within a school or district, be patient, be persistent, and be focused. Develop strategic plans designed to identify two to four initiatives for the coming school year. Figure 3.2 shows a sample professional development "blueprint." The following steps suggest a strategy for designing collaborative, ongoing professional development for teachers who are or will be using technology in a blended learning classroom.

Step 1: Pre-assess

Teachers should have an opportunity to pre-assess both their attitudes toward using technology in the classroom and their ability to integrate technology into their instructional content. They should set profes-

FIGURE 3.2

The Blended Blueprint for Professional Development

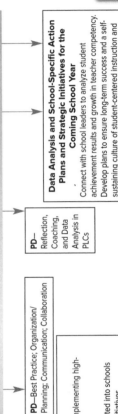

Example of a Blended Learning Professional Development Plan (Year 1)

Focus

Leadership teams develop PD plans that correspond with strategic plans designed to identify 2–4 initiatives for the coming year. Each initiative should have leaders responsible for its oversight and implementation.

Initial School/District Assessment

TIPS: Technology Integration Planning Study™ and Technology Readiness School Site Survey

- Identify current landscape
- Determine specific school needs
- Determine most promising practices
- Define/create systems to monitor the progress of each initiative

Establish Ongoing Classroom Observations with Pre- and Post-Observation Conferences

In order to identify what's working and what is not working, leaders must meet regularly with teachers to observe blended practices in action and determine which are gaining the most traction with students and impacting achievement.

Collect, Disaggregate, and Analyze Data

Schools commit to implementation of each blended learning initiative while consistently collecting and disaggregating data using existing and newly designed systems and Data Teams. Data is essential to ensure fidelity to the plan and determine future initiatives.

Staff Meeting Time

Weekly meetings keep content standards and teacher efficacy at the forefront of the conversation. At this time, teachers and administrators should be addressing trends, sharing ideas for best practice, working in Data Teams, and planning for the future.

Continuous Evaluation of Technology Needs

Evaluate emerging tech trends, analyze the implementation of current technology to identify successes and opportunities to improve implementation, and reconnect with the district mission/goals to ensure alignment between technology and outcomes

Ongoing Collaboration and Calibration with Colleagues to Ensure Alignment and Fidelity to the Plan

| July–Aug. | Sept. | Oct. | Nov. | Dec. | Jan. | Feb. | Mar. | April–June |

PD (2 Day)

PD—Introduce Initiatives, Pre-assess, Set Goals, and Model Desired Outcomes

- Define blended learning initiatives and develop a roadmap for implementing high-impact instructional strategies
- Align learning objectives with instructional methodology
- Develop technical competency using devices that will be integrated into schools
- Identify ongoing support systems to support blended learning initiatives
- Align the culture and vision while building a case for increased use of blended learning

PD—Best Practice; Organization/ Planning; Communication; Collaboration

PD—Reflection, Coaching, and Data Analysis in PLCs

Data Analysis and School-Specific Action Plans and Strategic Initiatives for the Coming School Year

Connect with school leaders to analyze student achievement results and growth in teacher competency. Develop plans to ensure long-term success and a self-sustaining culture of student-centered instruction and implementation of best-practice blended strategies.

sional learning goals that reflect their individual needs for professional development. Once the degree to which a school or district is ready to implement new blended learning initiatives has been determined, dig into strategic goals and discuss them with teachers. All teachers should identify what their own objectives are for their blended learning classroom. Objectives should align with the objectives of other teachers within the district. Planned outcomes for a blended learning environment in the classroom should be closely tied to student achievement rather than student engagement. Blended learning initiatives will provide engaging tools for the purpose of building skills and enhancing content, but student achievement remains the catalyst for change.

Step 2: Provide hands-on professional development opportunities

Not all teachers are comfortable with technology. Successful professional development should meet teachers where they are. To learn the relevance of technology, a hands-on approach should be used. Professional development experiences should be designed and delivered through a blended experience for teachers. When teachers participate as learners in the environment that they will be teaching in, they acquire first-hand knowledge to draw upon later. The tools of technology should be used in context to learning goals, ensuring educators understand the importance of why and how technology as a tool is best fused into instruction and learning. Digital tools are not "in addition to" traditional learning models for students, but instead allow teachers to replace traditional models of instruction with self-directed learning opportunities for students.

Step 3: Continuously model desired outcomes for teachers

Administrators, technology coaches, and mentors should model the techniques for achieving a successful blended learning environment.

Teachers want to know what blended learning will look like in their classrooms. During the first professional development days, provide multiple examples of what successful blended learning can look like with pilot activities and programs. Educators will have the opportunity to embrace innovation, seek new learning opportunities, and commit to the school's mission and vision. Create opportunities for teachers to develop a positive culture around change. Once blended learning environments are generating ideas, utilize examples from as many teachers as possible to highlight moments of success, which can then serve as models of practices that contribute positively to the overall culture of the school.

Step 4: Establish communities of practice

Set aside time during the week for collaboration among all educators across grades and subjects to celebrate and share successes, ideas, challenges, and frustrations. Engaging the technology together can offer just-in-time support for colleagues, and maintain the connection between professional development and implementation.

Step 5: Provide ongoing support

School leaders should meet regularly with teachers to observe blended learning practices in action and determine which models are gaining the most traction with students. If regular classroom observations accompanied by pre- and post-observation conferences are not already a part of your school's professional development plan, you may want to make it a part of the blended learning initiative. The most important factor in determining whether blended models of instruction are successful is whether or not they are implemented with fidelity at the student level. Observations provide an opportunity to evaluate implementation efforts. Subsequent conferences with teachers provide insight into how to best support initiatives as they move forward. When observations are used to help teachers make mid-course corrections and achieve better results, teachers know that the observing administrators are active participants in the implementation process, as opposed to passive observers of the results.

Professional Development Topics

Professional development is very personal for teachers as they develop their own learning goals and professional learning networks, yet there will be a need to have opportunities for growth that are guided by the district. The following are topics that could be considered when they correspond with the strategic goals of the district.

Data

Administrators who experience the greatest success in the implementation of their blended learning initiatives are also those who work diligently to ensure a handful of topics are discussed on a weekly basis. Data is a key topic to discuss regularly, and blended learning administrators should make platforms available that allow teachers to collect, disaggregate, and disseminate data for immediate and future use. The more actionable data that is available to Data Teams, the better teachers' efforts are supported. Initiatives that show a positive impact on student achievement are the ones that continue to receive funding. Data is one of the most important elements in determining not only whether or not work has been fruitful, but also whether or not initiatives will be implemented at a deeper and more meaningful level in the future.

Weekly staff meeting conversations should include discussions related to content standards, specifically the Priority Standards, and the ability of staff to link the appropriate blended learning strategies with identified standards in a given grade and content area. During weekly collaboration time, teachers and administrators should work toward addressing blended learning trends, discussing opportunities and needs related to their technology tools, identifying student concerns, sharing ideas for best practices, planning collaboratively, and developing strategies for the future of the school's or district's blended learning initiative. When these conversations are a part of the weekly agenda, they play out in teachers' everyday planning.

Communication in the Online/Blended Space

Interaction in online and blended programs varies from one model to the next depending upon a number of different variables. Interaction in a face-to-face program is predominantly based on verbal and nonverbal communication, while virtual interaction is predominantly written. Administrators and faculty should remain cognizant of communication differences and work to ensure that communication is clear and respectful, and that it matches the sender's intention irrespective of the medium.

Effective Learning Environments

Creating an effective learning environment begins with an understanding of how that environment might need to be adapted with the infusion of digital tools and resources. Walk into any brick-and-mortar classroom during the first week of school, and you'll undoubtedly hear a teacher discussing the rules and behavioral expectations in his/her class. These conversations are equally important in the blended learning model classrooms. Solicit feedback from students to create classroom norms. Faculty teams should collaborate through professional development to establish a standard of acceptable norms and behaviors in the classroom.

Digital Citizenship

Students today are navigating in a digital world without a compass. In many cases, their experience with collaborative tools, social networking platforms, and informational outlets is far greater than what the adults in their lives have experienced using the Internet. However, teaching students to make smart, safe, informed decisions about the content they create, share, or edit begins with adults. Educators are better suited to facilitate student understanding about the productive use of digital tools when they are good digital citizens themselves. As teachers gain more understanding about the themes of digital citizenship (safety, copyright, cyber-bullying, effective searching, Web site evaluation, and Internet privacy, to name a few) they can infuse those themes into content instruction.

Privacy Standards and FERPA

Important legislation such as the Family Educational Rights and Privacy Act protects student records and each child's right to privacy. Generally, schools must obtain permission before any part of a student's record is available in a public forum. Many teachers working in the online and blended learning space have a number of questions related to this topic. Addressing those questions proactively, during your scheduled professional development time, protects both students and teachers.

Personalized Learning

In a blended learning environment, teachers will encounter a shift to personalized, student-centered instruction where the learning objectives and content as well as the method and pace of teaching may all vary. Personalized learning is focused on the learner; learners have a choice in what and how they learn. There are many elements that come into play in a classroom focused on personalized learning (see Figure 3.3). Teachers will need experience with tutoring or providing one-on-one after-school help as they learn to use adaptive technologies to activate the growth and development of independent learners who set their own learning goals. Teachers should pre-assess students to identify what their needs are. Learners should be involved in the

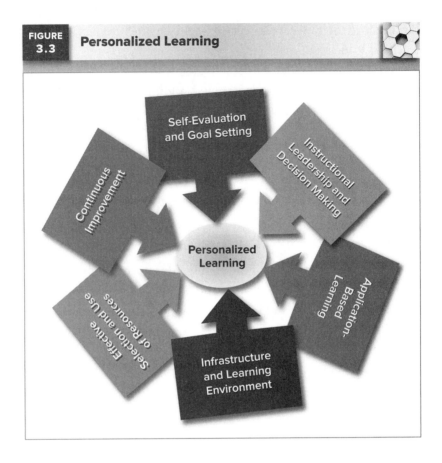

FIGURE 3.3   **Personalized Learning**

decisions about what they learn and how they are going to engage in the content, as part of the decision making afforded to students in a blended learning environment. The learner is responsible for the effective selection of tools and resources to achieve established academic goals. Students need to be aware of their own personal data and use it to guide their learning path. Professional development is necessary to support teachers in their understanding of personalized learning and how to effectively practice it in a blended environment.

Student-Centered Application-Based Learning

Problem solving is one of the most critical skills that our students will need in their workplaces and in their personal lives. Application-based learning experiences (ABLE) provide experiential *context* for the curricular *content*. These learning experiences can be in the form of tasks or challenges that require critical thinking, problem solving, and communication skills, and they are central to personalized learning. Tasks or challenges can be designed following the form of "authentic" performance assessments, project- or problem-based learning, or inquiry learning. The individual student's needs are at the center of the learning, compared to tasks or problems designed for the whole student group. Engaging students in utilizing application-based learning experiences in the classroom advances their digital communication and collaboration skills by putting the content in context and involving them in real-world problems that will require critical thinking skills and creativity to solve. For example, districts that utilize a rotation blended learning model frequently integrate application-based learning experiences as a component of that model. Authentic problems require students to apply their knowledge and access online resources. These tasks help learners develop information literacy that is critical to the ability to identify creditable sources and make sound decisions when evaluating the quality of information available on the Internet. ABLE tasks challenge students to collaborate with their peers to share and evaluate the credibility of their collected information. Collaboration leads to opportunities to synthesize information and transform collected content or data into a viable solution for the task or challenge being assessed.

A unit of study in the application-based learning model will have:

- "Unwrapped" Priority Standards written in student-friendly language
- "Unwrapped" interdisciplinary standards written in student-friendly language

- ISTE standards
- Essential Questions
- Big Ideas
- Scenario or task
- Supporting tasks
- Evaluation rubric

Questions to ask when creating supporting tasks include:

- What standards will be addressed in the subtasks?
- What are the learning targets that will help students know whether they are successfully meeting the requirements of the task?
- What direct instruction might take place either for the entire class or for individuals based on formative assessment?
- How will you help students to manage their time and resources during this project and enable them to develop these management skills for future tasks?

Teachers possess excellent content knowledge, and they are adept at integrating technology and software programs into their teaching successfully when they are enabled to use ABLE-style pedagogy. Implementation of ABLE will require teachers to participate in professional development activities to help them identify high-quality online learning resources and refine their use of approaches such as student-centered inquiry and personalized learning. Teachers will need professional learning experiences related to the acquisition of information literacy skills to critically review and evaluate the relevance and reliability of online information in order to guide their students to do the same.

Tara, a fifth-grade teacher, begins with a prioritized Common Core State Standard her students will meet. She also determines which International Society for Technology in Education (ISTE) student standard aligns with the learning activity.

5.MD.A.1: Convert among different-sized standard measurement units within a given measurement system (e.g., convert 5 cm to 0.05 m), and use these conversions in solving multi-step, real-world problems.

ISTE 1b: Engage students in exploring real-world issues and solving authentic problems using digital tools and resources.

She then asks her students to analyze the standards to understand what they need to know and be able to do. She guides them through the process of culling out the verbs and nouns with the purpose of having the students rewrite the standards in student-friendly language. Often, these student-written objectives can be put into "I will" statements. This process gives students the opportunity to understand what is being asked of them, and "why" they are focusing on certain assignments, projects or activities.

Student friendly versions:
• I will convert different-sized standard measurement units to solve problems with more than one step.
• I will use digital tools and resources to convert units of measurement and solve problems with more than one step.

At this point in the process, Tara shares the Web-based tools that will assist the students in meeting these standards.

She also presents the problem tasks: Our fifth-grade class is going to be running in a 5K race. We need to begin practicing and increase our endurance, starting with 1,500 meters and adding 500 meters each week. How many weeks will it take for us to be ready for the race? Use the Educreations app to show and record your work.

The class then works through this task. If the task were part of a larger unit of study, other related tasks would follow.

An example of a complete ABLE unit of study is included in Appendix A.

As the learning leader, it is important that the teacher understand the "authentic performance tasks" model of instruction, or application-based learning. The model is based on units or topics of study in which there is an engaging scenario connecting an application of knowledge and skills to real-world tasks. This application of knowledge is supported through four or five performance tasks, each connected to standards, skills, and Essential Questions, with effective instruction to support each of the tasks. Professional development and ongoing coaching in application-based learning is essential to the success of all students.

Long-Term Support

When they are guided with plans for the purposeful implementation of technology tools and high-quality content, and given the support needed for success, educators don't feel so overwhelmed by the new expectations of blended learning. Planning a blended learning transformation with fidelity means embracing the notion that teacher training and development is a priority, and that long-term initiatives designed to support staff development are a necessary component. Building on the existing skills of faculty, addressing deficits, and surrounding staff members with resources and expertise over an extended period of time helps classroom teachers develop the blended learning classrooms that will impact student learning. When administrators support the real work that happens in the classroom every day, teachers learn how to manage the new blended learning environment.

Fortunately, federal Title II-A funds can be used to provide professional learning opportunities that focus on pedagogy infused with technology. A teacher teaching in a blended learning environment would most benefit from professional development delivered in a blended learning environment, so they can transfer the experience to their own teaching. Some of the best professional development experiences for teachers learning about implementing technology in their classrooms involve first-hand immersion in the use of collaboration, sharing, and innovation. Team teaching with colleagues is also invaluable to help generate teacher confidence and guide the acquisition of instructional expertise in blended learning techniques. The individuals responsible for supporting faculty and staff development should be a consistent presence in district offices and in schools and classrooms where blended learning initiatives are underway.

Tangential Professional Development Topics

While the primary focus of professional development opportunities will be on pedagogy and content, teachers in the blended learning environment as well as a virtual learning space need a variety of skills in order to be effective. While technology is not the focus of the following topics, teachers are always learning (and teaching) technology skills in context with other topics. Teachers learn the use of technology tools in context, and not as a stand-alone device.

Data Analysis and Decision Making

Schools commit to implementation of each blended learning initiative by consistently collecting and disaggregating data from both existing and newly designed systems and evaluating that data with their professional learning communities or Data Teams. The thoughtful use of data is essential to ensure fidelity to the implementation and to determine what future initiatives will require. In both blended learning and virtual learning environments, individual and whole-classroom metrics emerge as important tools for monitoring progress and then planning action steps based on student achievement data. Equip educators with the skills they need to be successful in evaluating data to illustrate the progress of students over time. Provide a process to be used in professional learning communities or Data Teams to analyze collected data and schedule opportunities for teachers to meet weekly, or at the least two times per month. The conversations should be centered on individual student data. Not only will the data inform the progress and direction necessary for the learner, it will also measure the success of the active implementation of blended learning environments.

Facilitating, Monitoring, and Evaluating

Teachers in blended and virtual learning environments should be equipped with the skills needed to facilitate, monitor, and evaluate meaningful learning in a number of different environments. Some of these skills include identifying instructional models that best meet the need of the learning situation, increasing competency with the use of technology, and understanding the difference between chaos and collaboration in the classroom. Online and face-to-face instruction groups are goal oriented, inquiry based, project centric, and variable with respect to their size and objectives. Professional development should model best practices during both the initial seminar and during ongoing support.

Specialization

As technology becomes more integrated into learning environments, teachers will adopt more specialized roles. Experts in choosing digital content, experts in curriculum design with technology, mentors in technology applications, and specialists in student feedback will emerge. Utilize the strengths of these people by allowing educators to work more substantively in the areas where they feel strongest. In the blended learning environment, teachers can establish collaborative work environments where they are able to focus on their emerging skills while collaboratively using the tools and resources available to support them where they may need more experience.

Technology Competency and Basic Troubleshooting

When introducing new technology, support teachers by providing training opportunities that allow for the development of basic knowledge and understanding related to troubleshooting potential problems with hardware or software. When teachers are solid on the basic operations of the hardware and software, classes will run more smoothly, teachers will experience greater satisfaction, and the school IT department will be able to focus on more substantive issues.

Lesson Design

In the transition to nearly every blended learning model, how teachers will teach will be modified in some way or another. The flow of a typical day may change considerably, student pacing may vary, formative and summative assessment opportunities will be more frequent, and student engagement will look different than in the past. Identify instructional design models that account for these changes and encourage your teams to develop innovative lesson design plans. Teachers no longer bound by the traditional model of instruction will reflect this newfound freedom in their lesson design models.

Online Language Proficiency

The new blended learning and online educational vernacular, like most educational language, is filled with acronyms and distinctly different vocabulary. Give teachers the opportunity to understand any new language associated with a new initiative before launching implementation.

Knowledge of Content Standards

Commitment to high-level academic outcomes begins with a solid understanding of what the content standards are and where their place is in the curriculum. Knowledge of content standards becomes more important than ever in virtual and blended learning environments, because there are so many opportunities to combine standards-based content with technology experiences in the classroom. However, it's easy for the technology to usurp the standards when knowledge of the technology exceeds knowledge of the standards.

Technology Coaches and Mentors

Expertise will emerge over time among staff. Empower those who are finding success in the blended learning models to mentor and coach their peers. Teachers strive to build peer-to-peer collaboration coupled with opportunities for reflection in the classroom, and often achieve excellent results. Administrators can provide similar opportunities for collaboration and reflection among teachers.

Comfort in the Midst of Commotion

One of the effects of a new blended learning initiative is the commonly held feeling that things in the classroom are more chaotic than they were in the past. Many students may be simultaneously working at different speeds in the content area, or on different content entirely. Additionally, active discussion groups may emerge in a problem-based learning environment that make a classroom sound louder than it would have in a traditional lecture scenario. Silence does not mean progress, any more than volume means on-task conversation. Distinguishing between chaos and collaboration is a skill that may require time and training for teachers to develop.

Work Sample Feedback

Work sample feedback is often one of the most overlooked instructional opportunities in any brick-and-mortar, blended, or virtual classroom. Work with your staff to analyze examples of quality feedback to students for the purpose of developing and replicating best practices in the area of student feedback. Establish school and district-wide standards for what is expected of teachers, and then work with students to ensure they know how to receive written feedback from their teachers and use it to achieve mastery.

Technical Support Services

To make the logistical transition from traditional to blended learning as smooth as possible, address who does what with respect to tech support, and put in place accountability measures to ensure teachers seek out solutions that match the problems they encounter.

Empowering Teachers

A great deal must happen before we purchase devices and place them in our students' and teachers' hands. Simply having access to technology does not ensure academic achievement, nor does it ensure high levels of student engagement. As we develop plans for interactive blended environments, we must be purposeful and develop initiatives with student achievement at the center of all that we do. When we ensure effective implementation, we increase the likelihood that students will experience engaging, student-centered classrooms equipped with digital tools that support and enhance student learning.

Supporting teacher effectiveness through thoughtful planning and the implementation of a handful of priority initiatives is our most important challenge as we seek to positively impact student learning. Before we integrate new technology, we owe it to our students and teachers to provide a clear and focused vision of the desired learning outcomes that will take place in a student-centric blended environment. Moving forward, we ensure fidelity to our mission and vision by providing teachers with the tools and knowledge they need to be successful by accompanying each element of the transition to blended learning with very tangible professional development opportunities. When administrators and teachers know the blended learning models and the technology available to them, and have devoted the time and resources to integrate the technology in purposeful ways, they can make informed decisions about how they can best serve students on the path to meeting academic standards, and developing the skills necessary to learn and thrive in today's global society.

Teachers need to be supported not only through professional development, but also through a solid technology infrastructure and well-designed workspace. Ultimately, the success of technology in the learning process is dependent on the students' connectivity to global society. Having the ability to access content on the Internet at any given time is critical to success in a blended classroom. Professional development provides learning opportunities to be successful with integrating technology in purposeful ways when the path to the information is accessible. The adaptability of a school's infrastructure is what will unlock the doors to a connected classroom.

CHAPTER 4

Technology Infrastructure and Facilities

Leading a successful implementation of blended learning environments means aligning instruction and curriculum with district technology infrastructure and site facilities. Infrastructure is fundamental for student success in a digitally infused environment. Purposefully designed collaboration and communication between the IT staff, curriculum design teams, and teachers will help choreograph the student experience using devices and digital content to bring about the best outcomes possible. Imagine a train moving down a set of parallel rails to its destination. Both rails must be true for the train to move forward. Curriculum and instruction is comparable to one of the rails, and the technology infrastructure is the other rail. The students are the train, and the three parts will work harmoniously together as long as everything is in alignment.

The Infrastructure and Facilities arena of the Framework for Digital Learning Transformation (Figure 4.1) is meant to be a guide to planning a successful infrastructure to support digital learning. Today's school or district technology departments assume a much larger role in the education process than they did in the past. Not only do they support administration operations, the instructional technology staff members also support and enhance student learning through the management of interoperable systems for content access. As educational technology has changed over the past 20 years, so has the need for greater communication and understanding between technology support personnel and faculty and administrators. This chapter ad-

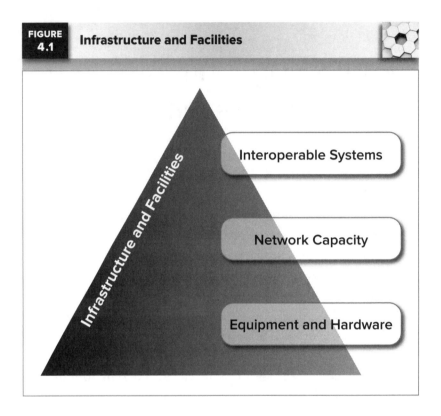

FIGURE 4.1 Infrastructure and Facilities

dresses the three key elements of infrastructure: interoperable systems for content management, network capacity, and equipment and hardware selection. But before focusing on the tools, let's consider the big-picture planning goals of aligning curricular content for student achievement with the technology tools chosen to support that achievement in a blended learning initiative.

Aligning the Educational Goals

A review of the educational goals and objectives for the blended learning environment is important before considering topics such as IT staffing, interoperable systems for content management, network capacity, or the selection of equipment and hardware. In past years, many schools and districts have selected hardware, created district technology policies and procedures, and designed networks independent of the educational goals of the school or district. During those initial years of implementing technology in classrooms, teachers and students worked within the parameters of what had been established by the school or district technology staff. When technology was in its infancy in schools, the use of devices such as tablets and laptops in the curriculum without pre-planning seemed to work. However, as technology has become more ubiquitous in schools, acquiring digital tools without first planning how they'll be used in instructional settings can often limit success in the classroom and the learning outcomes those digital resources can promote.

Schools will benefit from the updated Framework for Digital Learning Transformation and its procedures for the successful implementation of educational technology. A more open and collaborative approach to the creation and design of a site's technology infrastructure and its facilities enables the primary goal of student success as well as the goal of understanding the educational needs of faculty to ensure instructional success. When the educational goals and the overall mission of a school or district have been established, discussed, and clearly understood by both the IT staff and the faculty and administration, the selection of technology tools and digital content resources will dovetail with the educational goals of the school or district.

Consider these questions:

- What is the educational mission of the institution with regard to implementation and support of blended learning?
- What are the teaching and learning objectives of the teachers?
- What are the achievement goals for students?
- How will those goals be met?
- What tools will support the educational goals and objectives?

- How can the IT staff provide a successful environment that supports the educational goals of the institution?

- What online resources will need to be accessed?

- What kinds of educational activities will be conducted using the hardware (laptops, tablets, or smartphones)?

- How will the technology hardware use be supported?

These guiding questions represent a few of the conversations that should take place between the faculty, administrative staff, and IT staff. Under the models of the past, IT staff built a network that was secure and safe, and teachers and students studied and worked under the parameters of the network. Decisions such as what Internet sites would be blocked were made without collaborative input. While that model of design for infrastructure was sufficient in the past when technology in schools was minimal, it is not a model that should be replicated in blended learning classroom environments. For the most successful learning outcomes, it is important that all constituents collaborate to ensure that the educational goals of the school are supported by the technology available to students.

The Sandbox Analogy— Keeping the End in Mind

If students are given a sandbox and provided only with round molds to use to create structures containing angles of various sizes, the students, and the instructional goals, would be limited by those molds. Round molds may be safer, but their curved lines make students struggle to accomplish the assigned task.

If students beginning their blended learning activities can't access the network from their devices or if bandwidth issues create long waits for sites to load, or if some sites students need are blocked, disengagement and frustration may result. Strict filtering policies may not support academic goals. If students are instead given an open sandbox with a wide variety of molds and tools to complete their assignments, the possibilities for creativity and success increase. Tools designed and selected with the learning activity's objectives in mind don't limit the students. Inadequate bandwidth, unreliable Internet connections, software programs that don't run smoothly, or unavailable Web tools create a compromised environment for learning. As educators and leaders, we have all had times when technology has hiccups, and we have had to be flexible and adapt accordingly. But, in order for a digital learning initiative to succeed, the technology has to be planned to work reliably.

When key constituent groups agree upon an open sandbox environment, academic goals can be better supported. Identifying the tools faculty members will use with the students is an important component of the open sandbox. Policies and procedures surrounding Internet use and online behavior as well as the design of the infrastructure and facilities should be planned with the open sandbox in mind to maximize students' learning outcomes. Implications of the open sandbox paradigm are similar to the backwards-design model developed by Grant Wiggins and Jay McTighe (2005), where the premise is to start with the end in mind and then develop the framework to support the end goals. The end goals for academic achievement for a given blended learning model should drive the design of a successful infrastructure and the facilities students learn in.

Innovative classroom designs are quickly changing the landscape in schools. Modern classrooms will be technology infused, with gathering areas for group collaboration, couches and comfortable chairs for studying and sharing, presentation areas with projection capa - bilities, and study nooks for individual use. These student-centered designs encourage creativity, collaboration, communication, and innovation, so learning can be dynamic, collaborative, engaging, and multi-faceted. This classroom design model has a positive impact on student learning similar to the collaborative and innovative facility designs of many successful workplaces that exist today.

Key Elements of Infrastructure

How can school leaders and administrators ensure that the key elements of infrastructure are robust, progressive, supportive, and consistently operational? There are three key elements that require review as the infrastructure is evaluated and design considerations are discussed: interoperable systems for content management, network capacity, and equipment and hardware selection decisions.

Interoperable Systems

Interoperable systems manage the content, learning activities, student accounts, administrative accounts, and other components of the digital learning environment. Digital resources continue to transition to cloud-based technologies. Fewer resources and applications are now stored locally on devices, and fewer site-based servers store data and run software programs. The current and future location of digital resources, applications, and data solutions is on the Web—in the cloud. Cloud-based technology benefits educational institutions, as they will no longer have to purchase and maintain a large number of servers. Software upgrades are performed online through software providers, not by on-site technology staff. The number of applications and software programs that require installation on local devices is minimal; thus the deployment and management of those devices is also minimal. Moving to the cloud is a positive transition that greatly benefits a blended learning environment.

When implementing digital systems such as student information sites, subscriptions to online digital learning resources, or learning management systems, ease of use is an important consideration. Streamlining access to digital content is important for successful use. If students and teachers are confronted with a plethora of accounts and passwords, the likelihood that they will access their resources is diminished. A single sign-on that allows access to many online resources is an important component of a streamlined, user-friendly system. Students and teachers will only need to navigate to a main portal with one user account and one password to access multiple products.

In a blended learning environment, a learning management system (LMS) or a course management system (CMS) is often used as this single portal for accessing digital learning resources.

A learning management system is a centralized program that manages, delivers, and administers digital content, tracks student progress, provides assessment tools, tracks user data, and creates relevant reports. Most LMS systems are Web-based, providing ease of use for accessing services and information. There are many learning management systems available, and selecting one that best fits your institutional goals is important. In a blended learning environment, it is important to utilize an LMS as the umbrella to unify content that is being used throughout the school and the district.

Districts may use learning management systems and digital grade books from a variety of vendors to house their district-adopted curriculum and to deliver blended learning. They may also use the LMS to deliver online assessments to students in their districts. The introduction of an LMS has transformational capacity when classroom educators have participated in its selection process and received the appropriate professional development and ongoing support to maximize its usage in their classrooms. An LMS will typically house digital assets that include presentations of a district's standards-aligned adopted curriculum, supplemental resources, teacher lesson plans, student learning outcome mastery, and collaboration tools. Examples of collaboration tools an LMS may provide to staff and students include blogs, wikis, journals, online discussions, and peer review.

The ability of an LMS to easily integrate with other applications is important. District IT personnel should carefully evaluate the LMS to make sure that it is compatible with existing district-owned applications and applications that it envisions acquiring in the future. Integration ease is essential. A district will not want to purchase an LMS that is not compatible with its student information system. Thorough

LMS exploration on the front end will result in fewer unexpected integration costs and less performance disappointment on the back end.

Learning management systems can be either open-source or commercial. Districts should carefully evaluate the total cost of their choice and its ease of use before acquiring a specific system. While open-source learning management systems have the allure of being "free" due to the lack of software license fees, they are unlikely to provide the setup, integration, hosting, training, and support services that are available when purchasing a commercial learning management platform. Carefully evaluate the depth of the district's technology staff before considering an open-source LMS. If a vendor is not providing those services for the district, the district is going to have to either rely on the skills of their own technology staff or they are going to have to pay to secure those services from a third party.

A course management system manages course assets for students, tracks their progress, and stores their digital submissions. Students and instructors communicate through the CMS. While an LMS is similar, the CMS does not have the same broad functionality as that of an LMS.

A third, less often used system for blended learning is the learning content management system. This is software or an online system that allows the creation of digital courses using an online library of content to build the courses. Course authors, instructional designers, and publishers use learning content management systems.

Critical Components of a Learning Management System

There are multiple learning management systems from which to choose, and the differences between them may appear to be subtle. Some components that should be included in an LMS to assure optimal success include:

- Interoperability—API (application programming interface) type integration, allowing for single sign-on through a central portal (including Google Apps integration)
- Student information system integration, including ease of use in importing student lists or other class lists
- Ease of use for all constituents, including faculty, students, administration, and parents
- Easy customization and design capabilities for faculty class pages, with a content management system that is "drag-and-drop" easy
- Dropbox environment for submitting and sharing resources and assignments
- Homework annotator
- Assessments (quiz and test generators) with automated grading
- Relevant options for online standards-based or traditional grade books
- Attendance-taking capability
- Statistics for individual learners and classes
- Relevant school and district-wide reporting with meaningful data easily delivered in useful formats
- Customization of URL and LMS login page (splash page)
- Unlimited classes
- Mobile access
- Free or reasonable professional development and training modules included
- Responsive help desk
- Integration with Active Directory and LDAP, if used
- VPN access to school servers, if needed

- ePortfolio component
- Lock-down browser for testing
- Synchronous and asynchronous communication (e-mail, wikis, forums, etc.)

Prioritize the learning management system components that are critical or salient for your organization. Be sure to investigate data reporting options thoroughly to be sure needed data is available easily through the LMS system in a format that is manageable and flexible for your organizational purposes and reports. Allow time and resources for professional development to ensure that faculty, staff, and administrators are comfortable using the learning management system.

Network Capacity

The capacity of a school site's network is a central component in the success of a blended learning initiative. With a greater dependency on the Internet comes the critical need for adequate bandwidth. Most every person on a campus may have several devices that can access the network simultaneously: mobile phones, tablets, laptops, and desktop computers. With the additional bandwidth requirements needed for a blended learning environment, continuous evaluation of the data traffic and bandwidth usage must be conducted so that plans can be in place to expand the network as needed.

When considering network capacity, evaluate it from the following perspectives:

- Bandwidth to and from the Internet from the main data location
- Bandwidth to and from the Internet from each facility, campus, or building (WAN—Wide Area Network)
- Bandwidth between buildings on each campus (LAN—Local Area Network)

- Wireless access points in a building: number, placement, load balancing, bands supported (i.e., b/g/n/ac), management of devices, etc.
- Testing and mapping of the access points on a campus can provide valuable data, so this should be considered
- Updated and powerful switches and routers to handle the network traffic throughout the system
- Network design throughout the district and buildings, including existing subnets, dynamic or static IP assignment, and authentication procedures, if any
- Network security and data backup

Confirm that a thorough study of the network from these different perspectives has been conducted and the necessary bandwidth increases and hardware additions have been made to ensure connectivity throughout each building and on campus. It may be worthwhile to consult with an outside organization to conduct a study of the network and related bandwidth needs, both for current and future use.

Equipment and Hardware

Keep "purpose" at the forefront of all equipment and hardware decisions when selecting laptops, tablets, or other mobile devices to be deployed in a blended learning initiative. Educational goals should be the global common denominator for all hardware considerations. Before purchasing equipment, ask: What is the purpose for the device? What is the purpose of the educational activity that involves digital technology? What is the purpose of the mission integrating technology in the teaching and learning environment?

> Keep "purpose" as well as teaching and learning goals at the forefront of all decisions.

The Power of Community

Engage the power of the larger community of IT staff members, administrators, and lead faculty members in your school for research assistance, advice, and recommendations. Consider also including parents, students, and board members in the investigation of hardware decisions. Using their expertise demonstrates the value of their vested participation in decisions related to hardware. The blended learning initiative will benefit from their contributions.

Acceptable Use Policy

An acceptable use policy (AUP) will state the rules and regulations students and staff must follow in order to use the district-provided digital tools and online resources. Most schools have an AUP in place. Student-centered learning is at the heart of the blended learning environment, and an AUP should reflect this in its wording. Many districts are moving to the more student-focused term for this document: a responsible use policy (RUP). An RUP will provide parameters for using school-issued devices appropriately and the guidelines for safely investigating online digital resources. The RUP is best written in student-friendly language that is empowering to the student. Using "I will" statements promotes the responsible use of technology rather than invoking fear for possible wrongdoing. An AUP or RUP should follow the parameters of the Children's Internet Protection Act (CIPA, http://www.fcc.gov/guides/childrens-internet-protection-act) and the Children's Online Privacy Protection Act (COPPA, http://www.ftc.gov/enforcement/rules/rulemaking-regulatory-reform-proceedings/childrens-online-privacy-protection-rule).

Device Selection

Whichever mobile device is selected for use in a blended learning environment, the most important factor for success is not the device itself. It is what is done educationally with that device. How is it used to engage students and enhance teaching and learning? How is it used to create a robust and authentic technology-rich environment that supports rigorous curriculum design? It is what you *do* with the device that is important. The device itself is simply a tool that is used to help achieve instructional goals and objectives—a powerful tool that promotes creativity, collaboration, communication, and critical thinking as it fosters the skills needed for college and careers and promotes lifelong learning.

There are a plethora of mobile devices that offer a ubiquitous or blended learning environment. When selecting the device that is best for the purpose for which it will be used by teachers and students, there are philosophical considerations as well as hardware specifications one should review and investigate:

Financial

- Funding of hardware and devices
- Purchase options for extended warranty (inclusion of accidental damage coverage?)
- Devices—school-owned or parent-purchased
- Devices—option comparisons; purchase or lease
- Financial aid options to provide devices to students with financial needs
- Student technology fee to be assessed? If so, what would that include?
- Grant opportunities to provide potential funding
- Infrastructure renovations and enhancements funding
- Funding of potential bandwidth increases (monthly, recurring cost)
- Equipment repair funding

- Hardware refresh and future additional needs (funding and budgeting)
- Funding of professional development support and IT staffing

Logistical and Procedural

- Repair of damaged or broken devices
- Potential of self-repair licensing on-site (i.e., GSX for Apple, Self–Maintainer for Lenovo, etc.)
- Device insurance options (If insured, who will insure them and what will the coverage include?)
- Mobile device management system solutions
- Imaging of devices (reimaging, when needed)
- Remote access to devices
- Device backups
- Level of student and faculty accounts (administrative privileges?)
- Potential authentication systems, if used
- Timeline for hardware ordering, procurement schedule, imaging, distribution, etc.

Philosophical

- Implementation of learning management or content management system
- Online digital resources such as Google Apps for Education, Microsoft Live, Dropbox, Moodle, etc.
- Online digital subscriptions and learning resources (i.e., electronic textbooks, Discovery Education, electronic library resources, etc.)
- E-mail for students, faculty, and staff

- COPPA

- Content filtering

- Equity—providing devices for all students and considerations for students with no home Internet connectivity

- Responsible use policy (RUP) or acceptable use policy

- Consequences and handling of RUP violations

- Computer use agreement (or contract) for students, faculty, or staff

- Social media policy

- Digital citizenship education

- Rollout of devices (community event, beginning of school during class day, summer event, etc.)

- Faculty device deployment schedule (timeline)

- Initial faculty training and support

- Initial student training and support

- Information for parents (and possible parent education event)

- Potential security issues at school, at home, and for students traveling between home and school

If you take the time to investigate and make sound decisions related to these topics prior to implementing a blended learning environment, the effort will be rewarded with positive results, setting the stage for a smooth implementation.

Hardware Specification Considerations

As services and software continue to be hosted on cloud-based solutions on the Web rather than on local devices, the operating system or platform of a device becomes less important for accessing and using software programs. Some platforms or types of mobile devices tend to require more technical support and ongoing management than others when deployed in a large school community. The amount of time required to place the district logo or image on the devices and deploy the devices also varies according to device. While much of the success of a blended learning program is dependent on what is being done with the technology rather than on the device itself, decisions about the appropriate hardware device are important for assuring successful implementation. Here is a list of hardware specifications and mobile device attributes to consider when comparing mobile technology devices:

- Touchscreen or traditional-model device
- Laptop or tablet with apps
- Keyboard (external keyboard options for tablet)
- Operating system (some operating systems are more prone to spyware, viruses, and other malware)
- Hard drive or flash storage; size of hard drive
- Hard drive specifications (size, speed)
- Memory
- Processor and speed
- Camera
- Battery life
- Durability of design
- Wireless connectivity speed
- Included software applications
- Bluetooth and airplay capability
- External ports, including memory card readers
- Price—both for the school and for students and their families
- Ease of imaging, deployment, and overall repair and support

Keep the big picture in mind. Think about how all of the hardware and equipment will work together *interoperably*. Efficiency, streamlining, ease of use, hardware capabilities and specifications, ease of support and repair, and total cost of ownership are all important considerations.

Choosing the Right Tool

Smartphones
Recommended grade level: 7–12

Most students in this age group, depending on the school's socioeconomic composition, will already have smartphones when they arrive on campus. Many schools around the country have already implemented BYOD (bring your own device) initiatives with this in mind. Enough students will likely already have smartphones that could be utilized in small groups. Caution should be taken to protect personal information on the student-owned devices. Mobile devices are versatile, engaging, readily available, and active learning tools. Web access, text messaging, map features, alarms, timers and reminders, video and audio players, social networking sites, and downloadable applications can all be used to meet academic outcomes. Invite teachers to use applications that have already shown measurable results. When introducing new applications into the classroom, be sure you first identify the academic standard(s) the application supports, and plan to determine whether or not it is having a measurable impact on student achievement.

Tip: Shift from "If" to "How." Many schools still ban cell phones in the classroom. Whether the school has banned cell phones or not, they are there. Shift the focus from the question "If we should use them" to "How should we use them?" Capitalize on students' inherent desire to use the technology, and promote opportunities for them to use the devices for educational purposes both now and in the future.

Interactive Tables

Recommended grade level: K–6

Administrators can support teachers in developing collaborative learning environments with interactive tables, which have a multi-touch interface that allows up to eight students to work simultaneously on tasks that are inclusive, engaging, and highly cooperative. Teachers can make use of interactive tables to facilitate learning in a small-group environment with collaborative decision making. Many interactive tables are equipped with software that offers teachers insight into activity patterns, individual contributions, and completion of assigned tasks. This particular tool is specifically designed with younger students in mind. Its size, the available software, and its features are intended for students in grades K–6. Choose your vendor and device carefully, as some only offer software packages for children in grades Pre-K–3.

    Tip: Ditch the directions. A simple user interface is a teacher's friend. If the students can figure out how to use a tool without copious directions, then it is a good tool for the classroom. Teachers want to spend their time teaching to the standards, not teaching the technology. When selecting an interactive table, build on the technological savvy students already possess, and ensure the interface is easy for the teacher to understand and use.

Interactive Whiteboards

Recommended grade level: K–12

In much the same way mobile apps have shown promising results in research studies, so too have interactive whiteboards. With whiteboards, teacher support is the key to significant point gains in student achievement. Interactive whiteboards are the most underutilized tool in schools that have them in every classroom. Without teacher support, they quickly become glorified chalkboards, and offer no greater benefit than a standard whiteboard and a good set of markers. Teachers see the greatest positive impact when they utilize interactive whiteboards to create and display graphics and other visuals to students, utilize applications that signal correct responses, and are equipped with learner response devices. Developing the skill set needed to teach with this tool requires training, collaboration, coaching, and time.

Tip: Create control freaks. Make whiteboard purchases that include options for teachers to relinquish control of classroom technology to the students. Get it in their hands. Our goal is to move from a passive classroom environment to one that is interactive.

Tablets
Recommended grade level: K–12

Initially, many students will be challenged to view tablets as a tool for school rather than a tool for entertainment. Be patient, and have a plan to address this issue. Use the skills students already possess, such as the ability to embed graphics and photos, to improve student projects. Capitalize on their love of pictures and video to provide differentiated assessment opportunities. The possibilities for building schema around tablets as an academic tool are endless and represent a new frontier for many students.

Tip: Recruit student partners. Invite teachers to develop partnerships with their students in a way that allows them to share their gifts with both peers and teachers. This is a valid tip for every device. Teachers will find students well ahead of them on the technology curve. Encourage teachers to use student familiarity with devices as a vehicle for engagement. Students are digital natives, already possessing a wealth of information that can be used to enhance the classroom experience.

Video and Digital Cameras
Recommended grade level: K–12

Digital cameras are easy to use and, because most cell phones come equipped with both camera and video capabilities, are often readily available in the classroom. Because cameras provide instant feedback, there are countless classroom uses. Students love taking photos of themselves and each other, but there are also ways to use the technology for introducing new content, creating innovative assessments, providing visual representations, and promoting positive classroom culture. Reluctant readers or struggling writers can find a voice behind the lens of a camera. Students can conduct and record interviews to enhance an essay or project. Students can record themselves explaining a math problem or how to play a math game to share with parents. Students can create how-to videos or image-rich PowerPoint presentations. Encourage teachers to use video and digital cameras in ways they may not have considered for engagement, assessments, and differentiation.

Tip: Make sure it's not blurry. A clear focus on the content objective is essential when video and digital cameras are part of the lesson. Work with teachers to troubleshoot in advance how they will handle situations where students are not getting the best results.

Laptops
Recommended grade level: 7–12

Choosing laptops for a school or district is no easy task. Academic goals will determine in large part whether you should purchase laptops or tablets for your students. For example, if your school or district has a strategic initiative aimed at improving writing proficiency, a laptop will almost certainly be your best option. The keyboard and storage capabilities alone make laptops the best fit for writing. Laptops are more durable than their tablet counterparts. For districts that may not have the reserve funds to replace devices, this may be something to consider before purchasing. Other benefits of laptops include their editing capabilities, available storage (both internal and cloud-based), and the CD players, USB ports, and compatibility with projection devices that often come standard.

Tip: Know your needs. What's your school or district's Internet bandwidth? How much data storage will students need? Do you want their data to be accessible via hard drive or the cloud? These are some of the questions you should consider when planning bulk laptop purchases. Imagine buying a thousand laptops with lightning-fast processors only to find out that your district's Internet bandwidth doesn't allow you to capitalize on the computers' speed. What if you discover you need one thousand flash drives because the laptops you purchased do not have the necessary storage to accommodate the students' needs? Unanticipated costs can have huge financial implications and damage the credibility of a blended learning initiative before it has a chance to get off the ground. Recruit multiple stakeholders to vet the technology carefully to avoid additional costs you may not have factored into the existing budget.

BYOD or Not

Many schools and districts today are moving to a "bring your own device" (BYOD) or "bring your own technology" (BYOT) model of mobile technology implementation. In this model, students are provided with guidelines and options for the models of mobile devices that are acceptable for use on a campus.

District leadership should enact acceptable usage policies prior to device purchases or before any BYOD initiative is launched. The development of a device management plan will support a successful blended learning environment. School staff can rely on policies such as these to guide the management and usage of district-owned and student-owned devices inside and outside of their buildings and campus. Clear and concise policies will be invaluable to support the successful operation of blended learning. Implementation will be chaotic and confusing for all if policies do not precede devices.

Consider the following questions:

- Will students be permitted to take home district-owned devices?

- Who will be held responsible for theft of or damage to a student-owned or district-owned device?

- What school network access and Internet access will be restricted for staff and students?

- Does the district have an adequate data protection system to accommodate technology growth?

- What apps on student-owned devices will need to be available to them?

- What permissions will students have when they use their own devices at school?

- How will students and staff charge the devices on campus?

- Is there a sufficient number of wireless hubs to provide Wi-Fi service for the increased number of devices?

- How will the district protect the integrity of educational apps that they load onto student-owned devices?

- How will the district protect district- and student-owned devices from viruses that may be on some student-owned devices?

- How will the district control student use of the camera on devices to protect students?

- How will the district track the age and obsolescence of district-owned devices?

- How will the district respond to those families who do not own devices for their students?

BYOD Pros

It is of course more economical for schools if students bring a personally owned device to school for instructional purposes as opposed to schools purchasing, supplying, and managing devices. Another reason some schools are moving to this model is that they no longer see the need to purchase and manage mobile devices. As services and applications continually move to the cloud, school support of the devices is not needed at the same level it was in past years. This model frees up the technology staff to use their time and skills in other areas of technology support, possibly even reducing the number of technology staff members needed to support the overall program.

BYOD Cons

The lack of consistency among devices makes it more challenging for teaching and instruction. In a BYOD environment, students have multiple types of devices, and teachers may feel less confident in supporting the variety. Different devices have different interfaces, and some software programs may not be available on all platforms, or their features may be different. However, as services and programs continue to move to the Web, the consistency of those services across multiple devices is improving. School technology staff may not be able to support and service multiple devices. It is also difficult to ensure that students in a BYOD atmosphere have all required software installed on their devices.

The Foundation for Success

The capacity of a school or district to support an infrastructure invisible to the end user includes building and maintaining a reliable, flexible, and high-quality technology infrastructure with appropriately secure information and on-demand availability to all students and staff. The infrastructure should be able to sustain technical support; support hardware, software, and communication components; provide ready access to networked resources (e.g., LAN, WAN, and Web); and make assistive technology available for special needs students. In addition, teachers must be supported in their development and sharing of instructional techniques that can be customized for learner needs, as well as be provided with the opportunity to share instructional roles with their students.

Once decisions have been made about the design of a site's infrastructure and facilities, celebrate the success! Continuous reviews and ongoing assessments are necessary for the longitudinal success of a blended learning initiative. Benchmarks for successful implementation should be set, then plans for systematically reviewing, adapting, and sustaining the program are important for continued success in the future. Success starts with infrastructure and design that is aligned to the curriculum and instruction, beginning with a pre-assessment of the current infrastructure to be sure to meet the needs of the digital content and educational software that it will support.

Building and maintaining an infrastructure that will enhance learning, engagement, and achievement requires careful planning, collaboration, and support. None of that can happen without a thorough evaluation of the resources that will be needed to build that infrastructure. Financial matters are often at the top of administrators' list of considerations, but time (professional development, student scheduling, staff support) and knowledge (faculty expertise) are also valuable resources to keep in mind when planning for implementation of blended learning. A commitment to make sure the necessary resources are made available is essential for a successful transition to any digital learning model.

CHAPTER 5

District Resources

Technology has been called a game changer.

> *"In the space of a few years, and almost unintentionally, every rule in the education game was changed, so much so that we could even say that it became 'a whole new ballgame.'"*
> —Gabriel Rshaid, 2014

Once, kickball was the game of choice. It was easy to gather up a team and begin playing with only a ball and a few bases. Once the game of choice became baseball, more equipment was needed: the bat, a new smaller ball, and a baseball glove. The rules of the game are similar, but the technique is more refined. Connecting a 2½-inch-thick bat to a ball the size of an orange took some training and practice. The kickball pitcher is better suited as short stop for baseball. And the size of the field got much larger. As the bat and ball were to kickball, technology is a game changer in education. The rules are similar, but new equipment and a much larger playing field means learning new techniques in order to play. The resources needed to support these modifications make technology-infused education a "whole new ball game."

Districts support the blended learning environment through financial resources, personnel resources, content and curriculum resources, and the technology tools and devices made available to students and teachers. The Resources arena within the Framework for

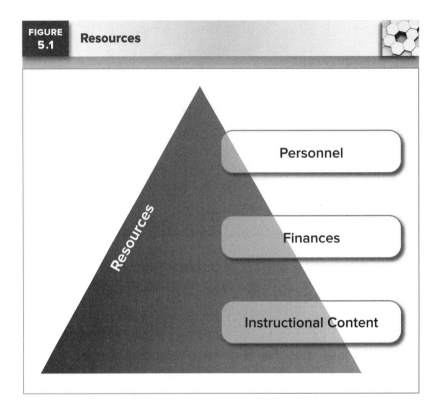

FIGURE 5.1 Resources

Digital Learning Transformation (Figure 5.1) helps evaluate the capacity of a school or district to provide teachers and staff with the resources necessary to support instruction and improve student achievement. Implementing a blended learning environment will require planning school district financial resources for short- and long-term funding for technology procurement, the deployment of personnel, and the procurement of digital learning content.

Financial Resources

Advancing a blended learning initiative requires dedicated multi-year financial resources. Once the models of blended learning environments are chosen, money will need to be identified for initial device procurement as well as future replacement costs, maintenance, and repair. Digital content will be acquired, and necessary improvements to the district or school infrastructure to support its use will need to be financed. Professional development for teachers focusing specifically on technology in the classroom will need to be planned for in the budget. Contributions may come from numerous funding sources to support a blended learning environment.

Districts searching for funds to finance their initial device purchases can choose from a variety of revenue sources. Project RED has estimated that it will cost a district from $100 to $400 per student per year to implement a 1:1 program (Rhor, 2014). Sources that can be typically used individually or combined include:

- Grants (e.g., Race to the Top)
- State technology funds
- Bonds
- Title I, Title II-A, Title III-A
- IDEA (Individuals with Disabilities Education Act) Part B
- Medicaid
- Corporate partnerships
- Foundations/philanthropic organizations
- Taxes

Procuring devices requires leaders to be mindful of the limited lifespan of those devices. While a grant may secure a one-time infusion of dollars to buy laptops for students, a long-term plan supported by a district's governing board and community ensures that a school has the resources to replace devices when they become obsolete. Technology acquisitions can be phased in by grade levels in concert with a multi-year budget. Permanent line items can be built into each year's budget to replace and maintain devices. A fee per student can help offset the costs of insurance and maintenance for purchased devices. Many districts charge $25–$50 per student, a fee that is waived for qualifying low-income families. School or community foundations can be established to fund ongoing technology implementation costs if charging students is not an option.

Districts that have a qualifying population of disadvantaged students may use Title I-A funds to purchase laptops or tablets in addition to curriculum resources and professional development as part of a comprehensive Title I school-wide plan. Title III-A funds may be available to procure digital learning resources to enhance the instruction of English language learners.

Poverty affects plans for blended learning in school districts. If a student receives a laptop at school, but has no Internet access at home to do assignments or view a teacher's "flipped classroom" video instruction, equal access becomes an achievement issue. Strategies that have been used by school leaders to alleviate this situation where it exists include increasing Internet availability to students by extending their building's after-school hours or by opening their doors on weekends to permit students to work on assignments or projects that require connectivity. The Huntsville, Alabama, district even placed hot spots on about 30 of its school buses, so that students are able to complete assignments on long rides home from school.

Leaders may be able to reach out to their broader communities to help them resolve student access issues. If various hot spots can be installed within a school's attendance area, students can log in to the school's network to gain access to their digital content and to their related assignments. These hot spots could be at the local library, a church, or at a neighborhood student club.

The Schools and Libraries Program, commonly known as E-rate, was created in 1997 to provide discounts of up to 90 percent to help eligible schools and libraries in the United States obtain affordable telecommunications and Internet access. Eligible participants include public and most nonprofit K–12 schools. Funding discounts that range from 20 percent to 90 percent depend on the poverty level and the urban-to-rural ratio of the population to be served by the program. Program participants are able to request funding discounts in five different service categories: telecommunications, telecommunication services, Internet access, internal connections, and basic maintenance of internal connections.

Professional growth dollars may be available from either federal or state grant sources for staff training. It may be possible to divert funds that were previously used to purchase consumables or instructional or reference materials such as encyclopedias, maps, or textbooks that are now accessible online by teachers and students.

Many rural or small districts have thinly stretched budgets and miss opportunities on products or services because they don't have the purchasing power of the larger districts. Expanding the use of cloud technology allows dollars to be saved and redirected. Cloud-based applications reduce the amount of time IT staff needs to attend to server and hard drive maintenance and replacement issues. Cloud-based applications also enable districts to buy subscriptions incrementally, so up-front costs can be managed and expenditures are better correlated with available IT funds. Cloud-based applications are attractive to districts not only for budgetary reasons, but because they do not require up-front investment in an application before there is a clear sense of how it will interface with other applications in the system. Smaller districts in the same area may want to establish partnerships or collaboratives to increase their buying power.

In the Central Valley of California, several small districts pulled together to create the Central Valley Collaborative. Alone, these districts could not afford the cost of a proprietary learning management system, ongoing support for that system, quality digital content, or the necessary professional development for leaders and teachers, and a few of the districts did not have the capacity to host the needed bandwidth. Through their collaborative efforts, they worked closely with a provider to fund all of these key components to support a blended learning initiative. Each district has its own independent vision and goals, but collectively they now have the buying power to pursue them. Each has a better chance to achieve a blended learning environment for its students.

Personnel

The greatest resource of a district is the people within it. Roles and responsibilities will change as the innovation of blended learning evolves. Creating a blended learning environment is more about the talent of people than it is about adding technology or devices to a traditional classroom. Seek opportunities that allow for the creative placement and use of talent in what might seem unconventional ways. Remake new roles and responsibilities to match the instructional models that are developing. A first step toward the transformation of a learning environment is to cultivate and promote team teaching. Teacher isolation will dissipate as creativity and collaboration begin. Teachers will gravitate toward the role that feels natural and that they excel in. Team leaders evolve into mentors.

The deployment of personnel will match the type of instructional schedule that will be the most successful in meeting learning goals. For example, if the rotation model were being used, the classrooms could expand physically, and the team of teachers could focus on different aspects of the learning process. One may specialize in working one-on-one with students or small groups while another focuses on the students' projects and portfolios or their online learning.

As students spend more time working autonomously without the direct supervision of a teacher, teachers may begin to utilize their time differently. When students are learning online for a portion of the day, time blocks become available for teachers that can now be used for collaboration or other teaching duties. Leaders can encourage and support teachers to experiment with schedules and to think creatively about the use of their time. As more students utilize the flex model, start times or end times may accommodate the shift to fewer students on campus. Thus, bell schedules may be altered to meet the needs of the new personalized learning structure.

Certain blended learning models will potentially afford school districts resource reallocation possibilities. The rotation model utilizes an online learning lab paraprofessional instead of a face-to-face teacher, and could realize a reallocation or savings of the cost difference between the two staff positions. As the percentage of student online learning increases, district savings could potentially increase.

There are many roles that may shift or become necessary in the IT department as blended learning begins to permeate the district. The IT staff should have a clear understanding of the school's curricular goals as well as its mission to support those goals for both teachers and students. With the IT staff as partners for successful implementation, teachers and students will feel comfortable reaching out for advice and assistance. The model for IT staffing is dependent on the number of teachers, students, and staff members that are part of the blended learning initiative. Following is a list of staff member roles to consider. A blend of technical support personnel and instructional support personnel is an important component of IT staffing for blended learning environments.

IT Staffing in a
Blended Learning Environment

Chief Technology Officer

- The role of the Chief Technology Officer, or CTO, is one of leadership for both administrative needs and the instructional practices of the district. The CTO is responsible for understanding the administrative needs for technology and remaining current with new technology options.

Systems and Network Support Personnel

- This team may include a director, whose role it is to oversee team members and their related responsibilities.

- This staff manages the servers, wireless access points, routers, switches, Internet service providers, and connectivity issues. They are responsible for procurement, support, repair, and replacement of the network and related systems.

- Members of this team are key to success at all levels. Their expertise and support are the backbone of a blended learning, technology-rich environment.

- This team is responsible for continued, ongoing review of network and bandwidth needs, hardware, and software, and must balance a fast-paced growth of technology with sound financial judgment.

District-Level and Site-Based Support Staff

- The staff members in these positions are responsible for ensuring that the technology works by providing ongoing and responsive support to all constituents in the areas of network connectivity, hardware and software, and printers.

- Some staff members in this group may be district based and may travel to a variety of sites and locations, but each site needs to have support available locally as well.

- This staff is responsible for the procurement and tracking of hardware to meet instructional goals.

• This staff is responsible for the repair or replacement of site-based technology hardware, such as projectors, laptops, desktop computers, and printers.

Academic Technology Director/Administrator or Team

• This leader or team is responsible for maintaining the ongoing vision and implementation strategies. This may be a single person or a team, but either way, must work closely with other academic leaders and administrators, including the curriculum and instruction leadership team.

• This person or team leads the creation and continual review of long-range goals as well as the monitoring of immediate successes, problems, and needs, providing options for solutions when needed.

• This position oversees the Technology Integration Specialists at district and/or site levels.

• This person or team develops a vision for the future in conjunction with other IT staff members as well as the school and/or district administrators and leaders.

• This person or team plans and orchestrates ongoing technology-rich professional development opportunities for IT staff members, faculty, and administrators, with a focus on the vision of blended learning (again, in conjunction with other IT staff members as well as the school and/or district administrators and leaders).

• This position is responsible for the continued, ongoing review of client-based hardware and software as well as online instructional services (in conjunction with academic leaders).

Technology Integration Specialists

The responsibilities of these staff members include:

- Professional development training, including academic integration strategies, workshops, and the modeling of best practices.

- Coaching services that support faculty members in their blended learning implementation, focusing on curricular goals.

- Consultation with faculty members to suggest technology integration ideas and plans related to their curricular goals and objectives.

- Classroom support as projects and new technologies are implemented.

Additional Innovative Support Suggestions and Considerations

- Help desk support, both live and virtual. Many districts and schools have technology help desks staffed by a person or team on the school site that the faculty, staff, and students can approach openly at almost any time during the regular school day to obtain assistance with their technology needs.

- Student IT groups and support "helpers" can also be utilized. With adequate instruction and clear expectations of support needs, students can provide a great deal of support to both the constituents as well as the IT staff. Additionally, it is a great way to engage students and potentially help them experience what a career in the field of technology could entail.

- A "Web help desk" or "ticket system" is extremely beneficial to the IT staff. Faculty, staff, and students can submit support requests online, which provides both efficient and streamlined support as well as support request data that can be analyzed for future growth and adjusted responsibilities.

• Virtual office hours can be provided to both faculty and students in an effort to ensure their needs are met during times outside the normal school day. There are several models of virtual office hours one could deploy depending on the needs of the constituents and the availability of technology staff members to provide the support outside regular school hours.

While there can be many titles and divisions of responsibility, every situation is unique and lines between positions may become blurred. Plan for the support needed at each site and create a framework for IT staff divisions. Communicate the responsibilities of each team member to all the IT staff members. Building a sense of camaraderie and teamwork among IT staff members is powerful. The IT world is changing fast, and can be problematic by nature and sometimes stressful. Acknowledge the expertise and wisdom of each team member, and encourage the open discussion of ideas, problems, and solutions, so every member can feel vested in the overall goals of the blended learning initiative. With a collaborative culture among the IT staff, faculty, school staff, administrators, and students, the potential for the success of a blended learning environment is greatly enhanced.

Content and Curricular Resources

Students may be adept at texting their friends or posting on social media sites, but many lack the skills to use technology as a tool for learning. It is our charge as educators to demonstrate to students how they can elevate their interests in digital communication and collaboration to solve real-world problems and locate credible information in our digital world.

Online Content

Digital content considerations go beyond graphics, animation, photos, streaming videos, music, and interactive multimedia. Content needs to prepare students for college and careers. Districts can choose from a variety of digital content as an integral part of their online curricular offerings, or can create their own online content. Creating online content allows the personalized alignment of digital content to standards and to classroom practice. Many teachers are currently creating their own videos for flipped classrooms, or to support lessons in a rotation model.

Whether to build or buy online content is a question that requires deep consideration. While students participating in the classroom, rotation, or flex models of blended learning will have a teacher involved for supervision and the delivery of instructional support, the remote, self-blend, and online models require students to be more self-directed learners. Some states and school districts are beginning to make successful participation in at least one online high school course a graduation requirement. This requirement is in anticipation of the fact that most students will need to take a virtual course as part of their college or workplace experience. States that have already enacted this requirement include Alabama, Florida, Michigan, and Virginia.

Larger school districts may have the capacity to manage and staff their own online curricula offered to students in either a school or remote setting. Typically, these districts will have their own teachers deliver the online courses to students. Students in these settings may have occasional face-to-face check-ins with their teachers or may participate in related course activities, such as a field trip to supplement instruction. Leaders considering this option need to be aware that a homegrown model requires a substantial investment of time and resources. Teachers will need professional development to learn how to create their own courses that include embedded links, resources, and online assessments. The preparation to develop the courses and prepare them for online delivery is time and labor intensive.

Smaller school districts may find it cost prohibitive to develop their own online curricula. Districts may need to contract with other content providers to deliver courses with vendor-employed teachers. The option to purchase online course services can be particularly beneficial for school districts that experience difficulty in finding teachers to instruct particular courses. Language courses and higher-level science and mathematics courses are usually the most profound areas of need.

Instructional Software

Choosing the content to support effective learning can seem arduous when you are considering all of the components. Seek software that supports the learning environment for the learner. It should be aesthetically appealing, motivating, and engaging. The learner should be able to see the work they have done, and what comes next. The ability of the students to choose their own learning pathways is beneficial. The software should offer immediate feedback and real-time data, and should provide opportunities for students to set and monitor their own learning goals.

Look for content that is comprehensive and aligned to Common Core or state standards. Adaptive software can adjust content delivery to the changing needs of the learner based on student response, and helps students pace their own learning. Look for software that has the capability to assign specific tasks to student users and that can provide valid reports of student progress and proficiency. Other key characteristics of software to look for include whether it allows for integration with a learning management system with a single sign-on portal and whether it is cloud based and has affordable, renewable licensing. Instructional software is available from a plethora of sources.

Keeping Blended Learning Alive

District resources are the lifeblood of the digital learning transformation. Aligning district resources is the first step to support next-generation learning. Remember, the learner is the number one priority when making decisions, whether those decisions are about financing the initiative, assigning personnel, or adopting digital content. Think innovatively to find money by reallocating funds or partnering with an outside organization. Classrooms and school calendars will evolve, and staffing needs will transform as well to accommodate personalized learning with quality content in a digital format that is device centric, adaptive, and engaging.

Technology in education is a game changer. And, as the game changes, to make our next moves agile and targeted, we must monitor our progress. What gets measured gets effective attention. So far we have investigated all but two of the arenas of the Framework for Digital Learning Transformation—pre-assessment and continuous improvement. Continuous improvement begins with a solid pre-assessment for baseline data. Proper pre-planning and ongoing support through monitoring for continuous improvement will get you started on the journey toward blended learning and will help keep you on the path in the future.

CHAPTER 6

Pre-Assess for Continuous Improvement

Engaging in continuous improvement requires work typified by regularity and consistency in a cycle that benefits from revisiting and refinement. Monitoring improvements encourages the cultivation of a school or district culture that fosters and demonstrates collaborative and shared responsibility for the success of each student. Continuous improvement plans attempt to improve processes that take inputs (e.g., monetary investments in teacher professional development) and produce outcomes through tests of measurable change (Park, Hirnonaka, Carver, and Nordstrum, 2013).

The gold standard of the Continuous Improvement arena of the Framework for Digital Learning Transformation (Figure 6.1) is for districts and schools to systematically provide reliable self-assessments that can be used to determine strengths and opportunities for growth in all district initiatives, as well as for staff and students. The data provided from these self-assessments should be accurate and available in real time. In addition, processes should be in place to use information obtained from data to develop or alter current practices to improve student learning.

Measuring what we want to get done begins with knowing where we are. It is important to pre-assess the current environment of the school or district by gathering and analyzing data, then prioritizing the results of this fact gathering. The data can then be used to develop goals, determine which model of blended learning is best suited to maximize student achievement in the district, and begin

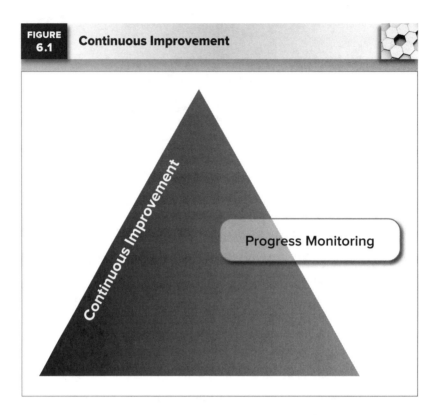

FIGURE 6.1   Continuous Improvement

implementation. Monitoring progress by continuing to collect data, celebrating successes, and being prepared to adapt and be flexible as goals are revised will result in ongoing improvement. Taking the time to reflect on challenges and accomplishments and communicate them to staff and other stakeholders will provide the motivation needed to stay on task.

A mid-sized district in California needed to know where to begin. The superintendent, new to the district, had a vision to introduce blended learning to create a more student-centric environment in which each student would have the use of a tablet or laptop device. A pre-assessment was scheduled to evaluate the current learning environment in the district. The pre-assessment data showed that the district had many goals that had never been monitored for progress. There were six large initiatives in place, and although the district had been working diligently to implement the initiatives, there was little to no evidence of growth or success. The pre-assessment also uncovered the fact that the intentions for student learning were not consistent among teachers across schools. Professional development would be a key component of the success the superintendent had in mind, but a strategy for aligning professional development with the identified technology and curriculum was not clearly identified. The infrastructure was insufficient and would need much attention before a rollout of devices could be successful. However, several promising practices were also uncovered. The superintendent found that leaders in the district exhibited excellent communication skills and that across the district there was strong parental support and involvement.

The pre-assessment the district underwent provided data results in key focal points: district leadership, professional development opportunities available for teachers and staff, the financial and personnel resources the district had at hand, and the capabilities of the infrastructure and facilities. These arenas within the Framework for Digital Learning Transformation gave the superintendent and implementation team the necessary information and data they needed to begin their planning. It also gave them a baseline from which to measure continuous improvements. They were able to prioritize the needs of the district and begin the journey of implementing blended learning in the district classrooms.

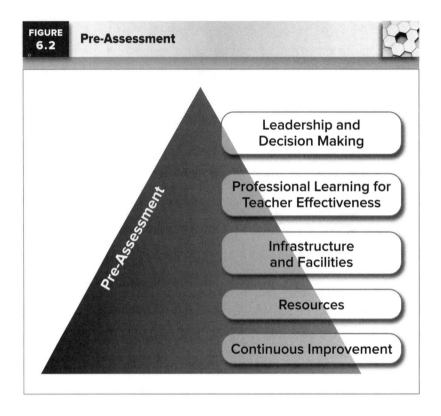

FIGURE 6.2 Pre-Assessment

Pre-Assessment

- Leadership and Decision Making
- Professional Learning for Teacher Effectiveness
- Infrastructure and Facilities
- Resources
- Continuous Improvement

Pre-Assess, Then Plan

The primary responsibility of a leadership team is to begin with identifying the needs of the district. The Pre-Assessment arena of the Framework for Digital Learning Transformation (Figure 6.2) is designed to help schools and districts figure out where they are so that they can plan for change. The district or school may have been making satisfactory progress with learning gains prior to introducing technology or a blended learning format, but adding the new dimension of a digitally rich environment will change teaching practices and requires preparation and planning.

Implementation decisions should be based on data, with the goal of continuous improvement once an implementation is in place. A pre-assessment should evaluate all aspects of the district's ability to improve student performance through the use of technology in a blended learning environment. To measure the impact of such a large change initiative will require a set of meaningful baseline data. The impact of the decisions made is best measured against an accurate assessment of the environment prior to implementation. You will want to know what actually worked and what did not; having baseline data prevents guesswork.

The pre-assessment will assist with the district's ability to:

• Document the current environment

• Determine the district's desired goals and outcomes

• Identify best policies, practices, and structures

• Report on current status and recommend actions

Sue Lemon, Assistant Superintendent in the Rosedale Unified School District, took part in a third-party pre-assessment study of the district's current environment utilizing the six arenas of the Framework for Digital Learning Transformation. Prior to the TIPS: Technology Integration Planning Study, which was developed by the author and administered by The Leadership and Learning Center, the district leadership felt confident about their self-assessment and they were preparing to move forward with a large technology initiative to bring blended learning to the district. Sue shared some of her thoughts about the process and the pre-assessment of the district (personal communication, 2013):

> "My prior concerns were more about content and using technology instructionally. What I found out through the study was that the infrastructure was simply not there. I would have spent a lot of money on resources that would have failed had we not

gone ahead with the Technology Integration Planning Study. In terms of content, we knew we had lots of professional development to do and we knew we needed to implement slowly. I thought we'd be starting to implement devices this year, but now—and directly because of the pre-assessment study—we know that we are not ready for that. The Technology Integration Planning Study saved us a lot of money and headaches, as well as saving me from having to go back to the drawing board. I was incredibly glad that we took a step back. Now our immediate concerns are around supporting our infrastructure."

Sue's district knew what they knew, and needed to find out what they didn't know. By taking a deep dive into their current school environment through a third-party pre-assessment, they were able to discover the things they didn't know they *didn't* know. They had been set to move forward with plans that may have caused frustration and could have disrupted the forward growth they were looking for.

Regardless of where you are in the process, if your district has not done a complete and thorough pre-assessment, you won't have the data you need to make the best decisions for your site. The extensive data that need to be gathered for a pre-assessment are best garnered by a third party for an unbiased view of the state of the district. Appendix B, a sample report of findings for a district similar to Rosedale, provides an idea of the amount of information that is necessary to properly assess your district's readiness for a 1:1 implementation of blended learning.

Gather Data

Data collected and analyzed over time inform the progress, success, and sustainability of the vision and goals of the district. The interrelated nature of the arenas of the Framework for Digital Learning Transformation results in a holistic view that supports the growth of the district's culture and professional practice.

There are many ways to gather data. A pre-assessment identifies both the quantitative and qualitative data in the district that are available to be analyzed. For both quantitative and qualitative data, there should be evidence and artifacts collected that support those data.

Qualitative data reveal the hearts of the people in the district, and can be gathered in several different forms, such as from individual interviews, focus groups, or environmental scans of the school. The interview process should include representation from all stakeholders. Individual interviews afford participants the privacy to share their thoughts in a way that they may not be likely to do with other stakeholders present. Focus groups can be developed with staff representation from the arenas of the framework under consideration. For example, when a district's infrastructure is undergoing pre-assessment, the focus group might consist of the IT Director, IT staff members, a curriculum director, principals, curriculum specialists, and teachers. These individuals will have various perspectives on the infrastructure and services that the IT department is able to provide.

Walking through buildings and seeing classrooms in action tells a story that cannot be understood through conversation or numbers alone. An environmental scan is a building walkthrough that allows observers of the learning environments to identify the physical assets of rooms or buildings and the ability of teachers or students to utilize the available space. These walkthroughs may be a necessary piece of evidence to either corroborate or refute information gained through interviews, focus groups, or data collection.

A district has listed 200 computers in each school, leading to the assumption that the district is on its way to implementing a 1:1 strategy by providing a device for each student and needs only to purchase more devices. However, the walkthrough reveals that many classrooms have only five computers and many are not turned on, and in some cases have not been turned on since the start of school. The computers may be surrounded by stacks of papers, or lack electrical outlets that are close enough to connect to. Perhaps it is observed that the two computer labs at the school have 30 desktop computers of varying ages. Several do not connect to the Internet and several are missing keys on the keyboard.

Observations of what the students are doing in the lab inform data that have been gathered about student learning. These observations provide the evidence that is critical to support the data. It is best if all data points can be validated, or at very least cross-verified (have more than one set of data to verify the validity of various interrelated data points). It is important to uncover all aspects of the arena being examined through the contributions of a wide representation of stakeholders.

Prioritize Needs

It can be overwhelming when the results of a pre-assessment come in and there seem to be an endless number of things that need attention.

When data are gathered and evidence and artifacts are collected, areas of need are highlighted, but what also emerges are the most promising practices in the district, and the opportunities for growth in each arena. When circumstances align to bring about the attainment of a goal or support improvement in an area of focus, there is an opportunity for growth. Once these opportunities for growth are determined, prioritize them and develop short-, medium-, and long-term goals.

Short-term goals will create some quick wins to celebrate, such as building an innovations or management team as described in Chapter 2, or an instructional (technology) mentor team as mentioned in Chapter 3. These short-term goals will then help you achieve the medium- and long-term goals. Short-term goals help build momentum and create opportunities for stakeholders to see progress and embrace the district vision for implementing blended learning environments.

Medium-term goals take time. They may take one to two years to achieve. Utilizing grant funding to begin or continue the purchase of devices and software is an example of a medium-term goal. Providing continuous staff development for teachers on accessing and using online instructional content is another medium-term goal. Updating computers or routers is a medium-term timetable goal. Many medium-term goals, including the examples mentioned here, are ongoing. After they are initially achieved, they must be sustained for continuous improvement.

Long-term goals are those that may not begin until the third year of implementation, or require that shorter goals be met before they are initiated. Adopting a learning management system, or updating classroom furniture to better meet the needs of the learning environment could fall into the long-term timetable goal set.

The pre-assessment may also bring to light the need to retool existing goals and develop new goals, which can help drive future strategic planning.

Use Progress Monitoring Rubrics

Monitoring progress requires the collection of data about the level and quality of implementation of each element of an initiative. In each

FIGURE 6.3   Sample Progress Monitoring Rubric Statements

Leadership and Decision Making

Shared leadership and decision making is apparent across all stakeholders.

Policies are in place to support the digital learning transformation.

Communication is transparent and seamless among all stakeholders.

A data-driven decision-making model is evident.

Schools and districts collaborate regularly to discuss data to inform decisions.

There is a clear focus on student performance and essential teacher knowledge.

Professional Development for Teacher Effectiveness

Students are prepared for college and careers.

Authentic/real-world application of skills is part of our learning framework.

Students are critical thinkers and problem solvers.

Instructional practices actively engage students in the planning and implementation of their learning.

Innovative learning methods integrate the use of supportive technologies, inquiry- and problem-based approaches, and higher-order thinking skills.

Assessment data are used to inform all decisions.

Students use their own personal data to guide their learning.

Infrastructure and Facilities

Integrated platforms are in place to support sharing of data and functional capabilities using Web services and business processes.

Applications are off-loaded to outside services provided via cloud technologies.

Some applications and content are mobile-enabled for a mobilized learning system.

Resources

Students have the best resources available for their instruction through innovative blended learning methods that integrate personalized inquiry- and problem-based approaches for deeper learning.

Financial resources are aligned with the district strategic plan.

Large purchases are negotiated with vendors to ensure the best price on products.

Online instructional programs are adaptive and use the results of the assessment as a foundation for instruction.

Projects are embraced because the staff understands the impact the work has on student performance.

Continuous Improvement

Community leaders track the effectiveness of projects while continuing to identify priorities.

Resources and facilities are regularly refined to help develop 21st-century skills.

There is an ongoing cycle of planning, monitoring, and review.

Continuous and ongoing evaluation of the data traffic and bandwidth usage is conducted.

FIGURE 6.4 **Rubric Scoring Stages**

District Resources: Instructional Content

Students have the best resources available for their instruction through innovative blended learning methods that integrate personalized inquiry- and problem-based approaches for deeper learning.

	Evolving	Developing	Operational	Innovative	Transfor-mational
APPROACH/ PLAN			✔		
IMPLEMEN-TATION		✔			
RESULTS	✔				

arena of the Framework for Digital Learning Transformation, craft statements from the guiding questions that your teams created, and use them as a rubric to monitor progress. Figure 6.3 includes some statements to consider when developing your rubric for progress monitoring.

Score Consistently

A change initiative will go through three stages: 1. planning and approach; 2. implementation effectiveness; and 3. results or outcomes. When scoring your rubric, be sure to score or assess each item at the same stage of the initiative. If the implementation stage is the stage you monitor, then all scoring should be done through the lens of implementation. Figure 6.4 illustrates the three stages of implementation, scored at the beginning of initial implementation.

Examining instructional content in the arena of resources (as depicted in Figure 6.4), a district might find that they have great plans to use digital instructional resources that will support personalized learning. They have realized, through their pre-assessment of district readiness, that these plans did not have a time element attached to the goals, nor did they include adaptive learning technology. Their planning would be rated as "operational." They realize they have more to think about and more planning needs to happen before they reach their goal of personalized learning.

The implementation of this plan has just been started. The first pilot classes have only just begun. The pilot classes show the development of plans and are a first step, but do not represent a district-wide successful implementation. Therefore the "developing" rank would best fit the implementation of the plans.

All students throughout the district are not utilizing the best digital resources available for a blended learning experience. The results of the plan have yet to be seen. Consequently, the results are still at the "evolving" stage.

In this rather simplistic example, the three stages of the change initiative were assessed independently of each other, thus giving the district a precise view of the current landscape of this particular goal. This microscopic view will then lead to the development of very specific short-, medium- and long-term goals and the action steps to achieve them.

The innovations team or program management team should lead the effort of mining the data for progress to discover what is working and what is not working. But data analysis shouldn't stop there. Dig deep to find out why implementations are working or not. Then adjust goals and keep moving forward.

Celebrate Immediate Results
for Quick Wins

Real transformation takes time. Expectations are often high, and stakeholders are impatient to see results. While your sights are set on the long-term accomplishments, short-term goals are necessary so that achievements can be celebrated as a way to build momentum. Kotter (1996) suggests that momentum builds as people see positive outcomes in a relatively short period of time. Individuals who are skeptical (we know they exist) will begin to see the results of their efforts, and their skepticism will lessen. Those that are moving forward will feel compelled to continue on. Reeves (2009) recommends looking for ways to create opportunities for short-term wins. Celebrate successes and build in opportunities for success—goals that you know you will meet. Communicate these successes to all stakeholders. We often spend too much time admiring the problems. It's important to learn from mistakes and celebrate even the little wins.

Be Adaptable

You've heard it before, and it's true: you must plan your work and work your plan. However, if working your plan is to the detriment of meeting your goals, give yourself permission to make changes to the plan. Instead of a rule follower, be an innovator. When you want to say no to something, stop and think about what that might mean. A relevant proverb comes to mind: Those who are flexible do not get bent out of shape.

Are there mid-course corrections that need to occur? Are you seeing a change in teaching and learning? Are students more engaged in deeper learning? What are the data telling you? Data are vital to measure the impact or effect of the initiative. Does the goal need to be revisited, rethought, or rewritten?

To keep implementation processes from becoming stagnant, review data and make adjustments on a bimonthly basis. Be sure to differentiate between different causes. If the blended learning initiative is not working as desired it could be because the implementation is ineffective, or it could be because the initiative needs to be reworked. Flexibility allows for adaptability.

Take Time for Reflection

Reflective practice may be the most important aspect of accountability. Reflection provides evidence for thinking and reasoning. The act of reflecting will ensure that strategies and implementations can be thoroughly processed and made part of the fabric of the school instead of being merely a series of disconnected innovations.

As an innovative leader, take time to reflect on the process. When reflections are captured and communicated to all parties, effective, meaningful dissemination can occur. A superintendent's or principal's blog is a fantastic way to establish a relationship with your community while keeping stakeholders abreast of the challenges and successes of ongoing initiatives. Sharing your thoughts, concerns, and celebrations is also a great way to document the journey and the learning that is happening in your school or district.

Be the Change

Facilitating the transformation of a traditional school system into an environment that embraces technology to support the cognitive complexity of students' day-to-day work so that they are deepening their thinking and learning takes innovative action. Everyone involved will need to be open to new ideas. Leaders will need to model their expectations, embrace creative thinking, encourage collaboration, be open to feedback, trust their staff, take risks, reflect, share responsibility, and perhaps most difficult of all, embrace the technology and new instructional paradigms themselves.

To facilitate blended learning, you must become a digital citizen. You must recognize that everyone has a voice, and should be heard. Inspire and influence others through example. You are not in this alone. This is an exciting time in education; find joy in the journey. Be the agent of change.

Application-Based Learning Experience (ABLE) Unit of Study: "Mega States"

Priority Standards	• CCSS.ELA-Literacy.RI.5.7: Draw on information from multiple print or digital sources, demonstrating the ability to locate an answer to a question quickly or to solve a problem efficiently. • CCSS.ELA-Literacy.RI.5.9: Integrate information from several texts on the same topic in order to write or speak about the subject knowledgeably. • CCSS.ELA-Literacy.W.5.1: Write opinion pieces on topics or texts, supporting a point of view with reasons and information. • CCSS.ELA-Literacy.W.5.4: Produce clear and coherent writing in which the development and organization are appropriate to task, purpose, and audience. (Grade-specific expectations for writing types are defined in standards 1–3 above.) • CCSS.ELA-Literacy.W.5.8: Recall relevant information from experiences or gather relevant information from print and digital sources; summarize or paraphrase information in notes and finished work, and provide a list of sources. • CCSS.ELA-Literacy.W.5.9: Draw evidence from literary or informational texts to support analysis, reflection, and research.
Interdisciplinary Standards	• National Geography Standard 3: How to analyze the spatial organization of people, places, and environments on Earth's surface. • National Geography Standard 5: Understand that people create regions to interpret Earth's complexity. • National Geography Standard 9: Understand the characteristics, distribution, and migration of human populations on Earth's surface.
ISTE Standards	• ISTE 2.b: Communicate information and ideas effectively to multiple audiences using a variety of media and formats. • ISTE 3: Students apply digital tools to gather, evaluate, and use information. • ISTE 4: Students use critical thinking skills to plan and conduct research, manage projects, solve problems, and make informed decisions using appropriate digital tools and resources.

Scenario/Task	The United States government has decided that managing the 50 states is too complicated. As a result, they have decided to keep Alaska and Hawaii as separate states, but are going to combine the 48 contiguous states into 16 Mega States that combine three existing states into one single state. You have been selected to submit a proposal for a new Mega State to the Federal Consolidation Committee. This proposal should include facts, symbols, and a persuasive presentation about your new Mega State. You must decide the format for your presentation, but the persuasive piece must include a written persuasive proposal. Facts may include: • geographic features (landforms, natural resources) • symbols (i.e., flag, motto, bird, animal, flower) • data (population, economic, location) Persuasive presentation may include: • What is your state's identity? • Why should your Mega State be chosen over others? • What are the counterarguments to the selection of your state and how will you address those?

Essential Questions	**Big Ideas**
How can using appeals to emotion as well as intellect persuade people to believe or act in a way that you desire?	People make decisions based on what they think *and* how they feel about something.
How does the combination of geography, facts, and history influence a region's identity?	Places in the world have identities that are created by their location, their people, and their history.
How can I use the Internet to apply my learning by finding and using information in my presentation?	Effective organization, evaluation, and searching will help me to apply my learning.

Task	Supporting Task Title/Description
Task 1	**Creating the Mega State**: Through research and effective questioning, students will select three bordering states to combine into a Mega State. They will then present this for approval using a medium of their choice.
Task 2	**Gathering and Analyzing Information**: Students will research the states that make up their Mega State and through analysis of data will begin to find connections, comparisons, differences, and relationships.
Task 3	**Creating a Persuasive Proposal**: Students will create a written persuasive proposal for the Federal Consolidation Committee.
Task 4	**Selecting the Presentation Format and Storyboarding the Final Product**: Students will explore options for presentation, select their tool of choice, and submit a storyboard (planning sheet) to their teacher for approval.
Task 5	**Final Creation and Presentation of Proposal**: Upon approval of the storyboard, students will complete the presentation, finalize the written proposal, and present it to the "committee."

SLIM Supporting Tasks
for Task 1: Creating the Mega State

The first step in developing your proposal is choosing the three states you would like to combine into a Mega State. However, you can't just choose any states. They need to be connected by a current political border and must not eliminate another bordering state from being part of another Mega State (e.g., you can't leave Maine unconnected to any other states).

Also, there has to be a reason for your choice of states. You need to research the states to find out what characteristics in their geography, history or identity might make them a good Mega State.

You then need to submit this to the Preliminary Review Committee (your teacher) for approval. Your submission can be in any format that requires speaking or writing, but must include the evidence (facts) and justification (reasoning) for the states you chose.

Element	Details
S What **standards** will be addressed in this subtask? (Include core, interdisciplinary and ISTE standards)	• CCSS.ELA-Literacy.RI.5.9: Integrate information from several texts on the same topic in order to write or speak about the subject knowledgeably. • CCSS.ELA-Literacy.W.5.9: Draw evidence from literary or informational texts to support analysis, reflection, and research. • National Geography Standard 3: How to analyze the spatial organization of people, places, and environments on Earth's surface. • ISTE Standard 3: Students apply digital tools to gather, evaluate, and use information.
L What are the **learning targets** that will help students know whether they are successfully meeting the requirements of the task?	• I can use different sources to get the information I need. • I can identify the political boundaries that divide up the United States. • I can use digital tools to gather, organize, and use information. • I can identify common attributes of states. • I can select an appropriate tool to present my ideas. • I can clearly support my ideas with facts and evidence.
I What direct **instruction** might take place either for the entire class or for individuals based on formative assessment?	• **Effective Searching**: Introduce, review, or reinforce strong searching and Web site evaluation skills. • **Map Reading**: Ensure students know how to identify landforms and physical attributes of a region using a physical map. Also help students understand that political boundaries often have connections to physical attributes of a geographical region. • **Claims, Evidence, and Reasoning:** Provide students with instruction in and possibly graphic organizers for organizing their writing/speaking piece. Ensure that they know the difference between these three parts of the assignment.
M How will you help students to **manage** their time and resources during this project and enable them to develop these management skills for future tasks?	• **Organization**: Help students develop methods for organizing the information they find using digital (e.g., Evernote, Google Docs) and traditional (e.g., notecards, journals) tools. • **Time Management**: Break the task into parts and aid students in putting each part on the calendar to meet the required completion date. • **Tool Choice**: Aid students in making decisions regarding the most effective use of tools for their abilities and learning style, keeping in mind the overall project. Possibly provide a list of tools appropriate for this task.

Task Evaluation Rubric

	Exemplary	Good	Fair	Must Redo
Geographical Understandings	Combined states are currently connected by a political border and allow for other Mega State options.	Combined states are currently connected by a political border and don't isolate any current states.	Combined states are connected by a political border.	Combined states are not connected by a political border.
Information Literacy	Sources chosen were effective for completion of task and included a variety of media.	Sources chosen were effective for completion of task.	Sources chosen were somewhat effective for completion of task.	Sources chosen were not effective for completion of task.
Writing or Speaking	Preliminary proposal of Mega State includes very thoughtful reasoning and justification for choice and demonstrates excellent understanding of overall project.	Preliminary proposal of Mega State includes sound evidence and justification for choice. There is some connection to the project as a whole.	Preliminary proposal of Mega State includes some evidence and justification for choice.	Preliminary proposal of Mega State includes inadequate evidence and/or justification for choice.
Technology Usage	Student tool choice is effective for task and demonstrates long-term plan for presentation of entire proposal.	Student chose effective tools to use in presentation and justification of Mega State choice.	Student tool choice was somewhat ineffective in presentation and justification of Mega State choice.	Student tool choice was ineffective in presentation and justification of Mega State choice.

Technology Integration Planning Study, Sample Pre-Assessment Report (Condensed)

TIPS:
Technology Integration Planning Study

Central District

EXECUTIVE SUMMARY

This Executive Summary provides an overview of the TIPS: Technology Integration Planning Study™ conducted by The Leadership and Learning Center (The Center). A team of four Professional Development Associates was invited to spend four days in Central District determining the district's overall readiness to support student achievement though the deployment of technology-supported curriculum, technology-rich instructional strategies, and technology-driven processes. During that time, team members held focused meetings, visited schools and departments, examined district artifacts, studied district processes, and interviewed senior leaders, staff, and community members.

The TIPS: Technology Integration Planning Study™, a proven methodology based on The Center's Framework for Digital Learning Transformation, was used to assess five major arenas referred to in this report as Study Arenas: Leadership and Decision Making; Learning and Development for Teacher Effectiveness; Infrastructure and Facilities; Resources; and Continuous Improvement. Utilizing the structured methodology, the TIPS team members:

- documented the current environment
- determined the district's desired goals and outcomes
- identified best-of-breed policies, practices, and structures
- reported on current status and recommended actions

The TIPS team identified commendations and most promising practices as follows:

- Student-centered leaders exhibited excellent communication skills.
- The Technology Department reported to the Associate Superintendent, who oversees Curriculum and Instruction.
- A culture of mutual respect was observable.
- A shared vision was communicated throughout Central District.
- Collaborative decision-making processes were progressing.

Opportunities for Growth for Central District were identified in four areas. An Opportunity for Growth (OFG) is a chance or set of circumstances that come together to bring about the attainment of a goal or support improvement in an area of focus. A timely OFG that is intently focused on a desired outcome can bring the greatest results to Central District. The OFGs are categorized by areas as follows:

- In the area of planning for technology:
  - technology infrastructure
  - expanded use of technology by students (i.e., BYOD, 1:1 laptops, tablets, learning management system)
- In the area of existing technology:
  - district-wide adherence to the acceptable use policy (AUP)
  - plans and processes for hardware protection, safety, and security
- In the area of integration of technology in curriculum and instruction:
  - Common Core–aligned instructional materials and digital assets in classrooms
- In the area of instructional leadership:
  - stakeholder feedback
  - transitional opportunities for new administrators
  - inclusion of measurable elements in the District Strategic Plan (DSP)
  - teacher professional development for the integration of technology and instruction

In support of these four areas, the team has developed short-, medium-, and long-term recommendations for the district's consideration. These can be found in the Study Recommendations section near the end of this report. Based on the evidence and artifacts collected, the Commendations and Most Promising Practices as well as the Opportunities for Growth are intended to be beneficial in the district's implementation of its strategic goals and objectives. In addition, the retooling of some existing goals as well as the development of new goals can help drive future strategic planning, implementation, and monitoring for the highest-yielding results.

STUDY OVERVIEW

INTRODUCTION

Central District contracted with The Leadership and Learning Center, the Professional Learning Division of Houghton Mifflin Harcourt, to conduct a study of its readiness to support student achievement through the deployment of technology-supported digital curriculum, technology-rich instructional strategies, and technology-driven processes. A team of Leadership and Learning Center Professional Development Associates conducted the study using The Center's TIPS: Technology Integration Planning Study™ methodology to evaluate all aspects of the district's ability to improve student performance through the use of technology. This report has been prepared to share the team's findings and offer recommendations for the district's consideration.

PURPOSE

This study provides Central District with a proven methodology for the assessment of systemic and organizational performance indicators. The TIPS: Technology Integration Planning Study™ is based on The Center's Framework for Digital Learning Transformation. This study began with an Orientation Meeting for the district's senior leaders and members of the TIPS team. The TIPS team leader/engagement manager presented an overview of the TIPS process; the superintendent followed with a description of the district's desired goals and outcomes for this study. The study agenda was reviewed for all meeting attendees, and time was set aside for questions and answers.

DATA COLLECTION

The TIPS team was offered the opportunity to observe Central District in action. In addition, team members compiled data from surveys, interviews, focus groups, environmental scans, and any supporting artifacts provided by the district to determine their major findings. Both quantitative and qualitative data were gathered. Three approaches were used to collect evidence and artifacts:

1. **Individual interviews** with board members, senior leaders, district-designated department heads, department staff, directors, principals, teachers, parents, students, and community members
2. **Focus groups** representational of the Study Arena being examined

3. **Environmental school scans** using building walkthroughs and information-gathering meetings with teachers, principals, and community members

STUDY COMPONENTS

Data gathered from multiple sources was examined within the context of five Study Arenas: 1) Leadership and Decision Making; 2) Learning and Development for Teacher Effectiveness; 3) Infrastructure and Facilities; 4) Resources; and 5) Continuous Improvement.

ARENAS OF STUDY

Leadership and Decision Making: This arena helps leaders focus their efforts on a comprehensive integrated approach to technology-enriched teaching and learning. This includes a clear decision-making process, roles for key stakeholders, and the commitment of resources to support transformation throughout the organization.

Learning and Development for Teacher Effectiveness: This arena prepares and supports teachers to facilitate and inspire student learning and creativity and to design and develop digital-age learning experiences and assessments for student-centered instruction and full integration of technology.

Infrastructure and Facilities: This arena supports educational goals through district facilities and technology infrastructures, the interoperability of the different operating systems and software programs, the capacity of the district's network, and the human resources management systems.

Resources: This arena supports educational goals through the identification and provision of the fiscal and human resources in place to support strategic goals and educational objectives.

Continuous Improvement: This arena supports the development of ongoing, reliable assessments to use data for informed decision making.

PROCESS STAGES

Three Process Stages are used to assess Central District in four of the five Study Arenas (1, 2, 3, and 5).

Planning/Approach: In this stage, the district was evaluated on the success of the steps taken to achieve its performance goals.

Implementation: In this stage, the district was evaluated on the success of the measures and methods used to achieve its desired outcomes.

Results: In this stage, the district was evaluated on the results attained from the planning and implementation of its strategies.

PERFORMANCE CONTINUUM MEASURES

Each Study Arena was evaluated using the Performance Continuum measures. Both quantitative and qualitative data were gathered by the TIPS team members to determine a performance rating for each arena. The five performance measures are described below. The table following gives the descriptors for each measure in the five Study Arenas.

Transformational (5.0): A systems thinking point of view prevails in the district; this is the most favorable or desirable state. Characteristics at this level include comprehensive and fully integrated plans, policies, and processes. The components of the district's systems are interrelated and undergirded by a strong foundation of collaboration and group effort. Also, there is evidence of a high level of interconnectedness across the district. The stakeholders' teamwork and level of involvement result in the development and implementation of initiatives that can be substantiated by local, national, and international measures of excellence.

Innovative (4.0–4.9): A systems thinking point of view is firmly in place. Characteristics at this level include comprehensive plans and policies; integrated and widespread implementation; and results that are substantiated by multiple forms of data. Leaders and staff recognize, value, and model the importance of an integrated systems approach as evidenced in their planning and collaborative projects in schools and departments. Stakeholders are willing participants in district planning.

Operational (3.0–3.9): A systems thinking point of view is in place. Characteristics at this level include sound plans and policies; widespread implementation of systems thinking approaches; and the substantiation of results by data. However, there are some areas within the organization where integration and collaboration are not automatically part of the planning and deployment of district initiatives. Stakeholders are involved in some district planning, but their involvement is not automatic.

Developing (2.0–2.9): A systems thinking point of view is being formulated. Characteristics at this level include the establishment of basic procedures; limited implementation; and results based on anecdotal evidence. Some staff members can work easily within the framework of systems thinking as they involve others in decisions and move toward common goals. Others operate individually and struggle to work across departmental lines to include others in decisions that lead to the development and/or implementation of policies or programs. Stakeholders are sometimes involved in district planning.

Evolving (1.0–1.9): A systems thinking point of view does not exist. Characteristics at this level include a lack of clarity about what to do; inconsistency in implementation; and variations in results. There is limited evidence of communication and collaborative thinking among staff members across the district. Leaders at most levels of the organization tend to work in decision vacuums. Schools are autonomous and there is little buy-in for the district's vision or direction. Stakeholders are rarely involved in district planning.

TIPS Process Methodology

Performance Continuum By Measure					
STUDY ARENA	**DESCRIPTORS FOR EACH MEASURE**				
	EVOLVING (1.0–1.9)	**DEVELOPING (2.0–2.9)**	**OPERATIONAL (3.0–3.9)**	**INNOVATIVE (4.0–4.9)**	**EXEMPLARY (5.0)**
ONE Leadership and Decision Making	Autonomous	Systematized	Outcome Model	Transformational	Sustainable Change
TWO Learning and Development for Teacher Effectiveness	Disconnected	Needs Dependent	Standards Driven	Student Centered	Personalized
THREE Infrastructure and Facilities	Proprietary	Fragmented	Consolidated Systems	Integrated Platforms	Mobile Learning
FOUR Resources	Single Resources	Disparate	Minimal Integration	Limited Integration	Seamless Integration
FIVE Continuous Improvement	Isolation	Collected	Useable	Data Driven	Integrated

STUDY FINDINGS

Major Findings

Using the TIPS data collection methods, the TIPS team identified the district's commendations and most promising practices as follows:

- Student-centered leaders exhibited excellent communication skills.
- The Technology Department reported to the Associate Superintendent, who oversees Curriculum and Instruction.
- A culture of mutual respect was observable.
- A shared vision was communicated throughout the district.
- Collaborative decision-making processes were progressing.

The TIPS team also identified Opportunities for Growth as a result of the information-gathering process. These are presented below. An Opportunity for Growth (OFG) is described as a chance or set of circumstances that come together to bring about the attainment of a goal or support improvement in an area of focus. A timely OFG that is intently focused on a desired outcome can bring the greatest results to Central District. The OFGs are categorized by areas as follows:

- In the area of planning for technology:
    - technology infrastructure
    - expanded use of technology by students (i.e., BYOD, 1:1 laptops, tablets, learning management system)
- In the area of existing technology:
    - district-wide adherence to the acceptable use policy (AUP)
    - redundancy for critical systems such as payroll
    - plans and processes for hardware protection, safety, and security
- In the area of integration of technology in curriculum and instruction:
    - Common Core–aligned instructional materials and digital assets in classrooms
- In the area of instructional leadership:
    - stakeholder feedback
    - transitional opportunities for new administrators
    - inclusion of measurable elements in the District Strategic Plan (DSP)
    - teacher professional development for the integration of technology and instruction

More detailed information regarding the strengths and promising practices is provided in the Recommendations section. In addition, the Opportunities for Growth are presented in greater detail, along with short-, medium-, and long-range actions for the district's consideration.

Results by Study Arena

The TIPS team spent four consecutive days gathering qualitative data through focus groups, individual interviews, and environmental walkthroughs. The results are described in the individual Study Arenas. A further breakdown is made through the organizational Performance Indicators that impact teaching, learning, policies, and productivity.

Arena One: Leadership and Decision Making

This arena examines the capacity of the school/district, through leadership (e.g., principals, board members, and building-level teams), to operate from a shared vision of technology, characterized by the belief that a comprehensive, integrated approach to technology-enriched teaching and learning will improve student performance. Included in this arena are clear decision-making processes, agreed-upon roles for key stakeholders that include leadership and decision-making opportunities, a shared student-centered vision, and the value of the community's involvement in the future direction of the district.

TIPS team members met with focus groups and conducted individual interviews with the following participants to gather data for this Study Arena.

District and Community Participants for Arena One

FOCUS GROUP	INDIVIDUAL INTERVIEWS
Superintendent	Superintendent
Associate Superintendent	Board Member
Assistant Superintendent	Assistant Superintendent
Principals (4)	Parents (2)
Curriculum Specialist	
Parent Teacher Council Presidents (3)	

The TIPS team members used the following TIPS Performance Continuum Rubric to measure the district's level of attainment for each strand of this arena and determine the overall rating for Arena One—Leadership and Decision Making. Three strands are examined in this Study Arena: 1) Shared Vision; 2) Organization, Culture, and Climate; and 3) Community Engagement. Optimal performance in this arena is Transformational (5.0)—Sustainable Change.

TIPS Performance Continuum Rubric—Arena One

LEADERSHIP AND DECISION MAKING					
STUDY ARENA ONE RESULTS →	**← PERFORMANCE CONTINUUM →**				
	Evolving (1.0–1.9)	Developing (2.0–2.9)	Operational (3.0–3.9)	Innovative (4.0–4.9)	Transformational (5.0)
	Autonomous	Systematized	Outcome Model	Transformational	Sustainable Change
STRANDS ↓					
a. Shared Vision	Autonomous	Systematized	Outcome Model	Transformational	Sustainable Change
b. Organization, Culture, and Climate	Focus on Instructional Compliance	Focus on Collaboration	Focus on Collaboration to Improve Pedagogy	Focus on Instructional Accountability	Focus on College & Career Readiness for All students
c. Engagement	Isolation	Two-Way Communication	Shared Stakeholder Vision	Collaborative Strategic Planning	Strategic Plan Implementation

To arrive at the rating for each strand, TIPS team members used evidence and gathered data to assign a numerical score to three process stages: Approach/Plan, Implementation, and Results. Combining the scores from the three process stages determined the total score for a strand. Based on the rubric, the total number of points for each strand could be as high as 15 or as low as 3 points. The following table shows the district's rating by strand in this arena. The highest possible cumulative score for this arena is 45 points. Supporting details for each of the numerical ratings cited in the table are provided in the sections that follow.

TIPS Ratings by Process Stages for Arena One

LEADERSHIP AND DECISION MAKING				
STRAND	**PROCESS STAGES**			**STRAND TOTAL**
	APPROACH/ PLAN	**IMPLEMENTATION**	**RESULTS**	
a. Shared Vision	4.3	3.3	3.2	**10.8 of 15**
b. Organization, Culture, and Climate	4.5	3.8	3.8	**12.1 of 15**
c. Community Engagement	3.5	3.5	3.5	**10.5 of 15**
Cumulative Score				**33.4 of 45**

Shared Vision Strand (Arena One)

Measured within this strand is the capacity of the school/district, through leadership (e.g., principals, board members, and building-level teams), to operate from a shared vision that is supported by the belief that a comprehensive, integrated approach to enriched teaching and learning will improve student performance. This includes a clear decision-making process, agreed-upon roles for key stakeholders, and the commitment of resources. Following are the TIPS ratings that support this strand. *In a complete report, each rating would be described in detail following the table, but in this condensed version, these descriptions have been omitted.*

TIPS Ratings—Shared Vision Strand (Arena One)

LEADERSHIP AND DECISION MAKING: Shared Vision					
PROCESS STAGE	**← PERFORMANCE CONTINUUM →**				
	Evolving (1.0–1.9)	Developing (2.0–2.9)	Operational (3.0–3.9)	Innovative (4.0–4.9)	Transformational (5.0)
Approach/Plan				4.3	
Implementation			3.3		
Results			3.2		

Organization, Culture, and Climate Strand (Arena One)

Measured within this strand is the degree to which the district operates as a cohesive unit in alignment with a shared vision. People have a voice and decisions are made collectively. Every incentive or program is geared to improving student learning. Below are the TIPS team process ratings that support this strand.

TIPS Ratings—Organization, Culture, and Climate Strand (Arena One)

LEADERSHIP AND DECISION MAKING: Organization, Culture, and Climate					
PROCESS STAGE	← PERFORMANCE CONTINUUM →				
	Evolving (1.0–1.9)	Developing (2.0–2.9)	Operational (3.0–3.9)	Innovative (4.0–4.9)	Transformational (5.0)
Approach/Plan				4.5	
Implementation			3.8		
Results			3.8		

Community Engagement Strand (Arena One)

Measured within this strand is how the district assists educators with the identification and implementation of technology resources that support research-based differentiation and assessment practices to meet the identified needs of all students. Following are the TIPS team ratings for the three processes that support this strand.

TIPS Ratings—Community Engagement Strand (Arena One)

LEADERSHIP AND DECISION MAKING: Community Engagement					
PROCESS STAGE	← PERFORMANCE CONTINUUM →				
	Evolving (1.0–1.9)	Developing (2.0–2.9)	Operational (3.0–3.9)	Innovative (4.0–4.9)	Transformational (5.0)
Approach/Plan			3.5		
Implementation			3.5		
Results			3.5		

Arena Two: Learning and Development for Teacher Effectiveness

This arena supports the capacity to become knowledgeable and competent with respect to incorporating technology tools that will support 21st-century skills and individualized student learning.

TIPS team members met with focus groups and conducted individual interviews with the following participants to gather data for this Study Arena.

District and Community Participants for Arena Two

FOCUS GROUP	INDIVIDUAL INTERVIEWS
Associate Superintendent	Associate Superintendent
Curriculum Specialists (3)	Director—Technical Services
Principals (3)	Curriculum Specialists (2)
Teachers (2)	Principal
Parents (2)	Teachers (2)

The TIPS team members used the following TIPS Performance Continuum Rubric to measure the district's level of attainment for each strand of this arena and determine the overall rating for Arena Two—Learning and Development for Teacher Effectiveness. Two strands are examined in this Study Arena: 1) Student-Centered Learning; and 2) Professional Growth Model. Optimal performance in this arena is Transformational 5.0—Personalized.

TIPS Performance Continuum Rubric—Arena Two

LEARNING AND DEVELOPMENT FOR TEACHER EFFECTIVENESS					
STUDY ARENA TWO RESULTS →	**← PERFORMANCE CONTINUUM →**				
	Evolving (1.0–1.9)	**Developing (2.0–2.9)**	**Operational (3.0–3.9)**	**Innovative (4.0–4.9)**	**Transformational (5.0)**
	Disconnected	Needs Dependent	Standards Driven	Student Centered	Personalized
STRANDS ↓					
a. Student-Centered Learning	Teacher Directed	Differentiated Instruction	Standards-Driven Instruction	Student-Centered Instruction	Competency-Based 21st-Century Skills
b. Professional Growth Model	Independent and Site-Based PD	District-Focused PD Programs	Data-Directed PD Programs	Instructional Coaching/ Mentoring PD	Pervasive Professional Learning Networks

To arrive at the rating for each strand, TIPS team members used evidence and gathered data to assign a numerical score to three process stages: Approach/Plan, Implementation, and Results. Combining the scores from the three process stages determined the total score for a strand. Based on the rubric, the total number of points for each strand could be as high as 15 or as low as 3 points. The following table shows the district's rating by strand in this arena. The highest possible cumulative score for this arena is 30 points. Supporting details for each of the numerical ratings cited in the table are provided in greater detail in the sections that follow.

TIPS Ratings by Process Stages for Arena Two

LEARNING AND DEVELOPMENT FOR TEACHER EFFECTIVENESS				
STRAND	**PROCESS STAGES**			**STRAND TOTAL**
	APPROACH/ PLAN	IMPLEMENTATION	RESULTS	
a. Student-Centered Learning	4.3	3.7	3.7	**11.7 of 15**
b. Professional Growth Model	3.2	3.2	3.2	**9.6 of 15**
Cumulative Score				**21.3 of 30**

Student-Centered Learning Strand (Arena Two)

Measured within this strand is the concept that teachers know, understand, and incorporate a wide variety of instructional content and methodologies in their teaching. Districts must strive to promote the kind of professional learning for teachers that strengthens valued outcomes for addressing the needs of their students. The TIPS ratings for the three processes that support this strand are provided in the table.

TIPS Ratings—Student-Centered Learning Strand (Arena Two)

LEARNING AND DEVELOPMENT FOR TEACHER EFFECTIVENESS: Student-Centered Learning					
PROCESS STAGE	**← PERFORMANCE CONTINUUM →**				
	Evolving (1.0–1.9)	Developing (2.0–2.9)	Operational (3.0–3.9)	Innovative (4.0–4.9)	Transformational (5.0)
Approach/Plan				4.3	
Implementation			3.7		
Results			3.7		

Professional Growth Model Strand (Arena Two)

Measured within this strand is evidence that teachers know, understand, and incorporate a wide variety of instructional content and methodologies in their teaching. Districts must strive to promote the kind of professional learning for teachers that strengthens valued outcomes for addressing the needs of their students. The TIPS ratings for the three processes that support this strand are provided in the table.

TIPS Ratings—Professional Growth Model Strand (Arena Two)

LEARNING AND DEVELOPMENT FOR TEACHER EFFECTIVENESS: Professional Growth Model					
PROCESS STAGE	← PERFORMANCE CONTINUUM →				
	Evolving (1.0–1.9)	Developing (2.0–2.9)	Operational (3.0–3.9)	Innovative (4.0–4.9)	Transformational (5.0)
Approach/Plan			3.2		
Implementation			3.2		
Results			3.2		

Arena Three—Infrastructure and Facilities

This arena examines the capacity of the school/district to support an infrastructure that is invisible to the end user. This includes building and maintaining a reliable, flexible, and high-quality technology infrastructure with appropriately secure information and availability (e.g., user-friendly) on demand to all students and staff. The infrastructure should be able to a) sustain technical support; b) support hardware, software, and communication components; c) provide ready access to networked resources (e.g., LAN, WAN, and Web); and d) make assistive technology available for special needs students. In addition, teachers must be supported in their development and sharing of instructional techniques that can be customized for learner needs, as well as be provided with the opportunity to share instructional roles with their students.

TIPS team members met with focus groups and conducted individual interviews with the following participants to gather data for this arena study.

District Participants for Arena Three

FOCUS GROUP	INDIVIDUAL INTERVIEWS
Director—Technical Services	Superintendent
Curriculum Specialists (3)	Board Member
Principals (3)	Assistant Superintendent
Teachers (2)	

Due to the nature of Arena Three, the three process stages rated in the previous two arenas do not apply to this arena. Instead, each strand and its supporting sub-strands are rated using the following TIPS Performance Continuum Rubric for Arena Three. The rubric was applied to measure the district's level of attainment within each strand and determine an overall rating for Arena Three—Infrastructure and Facilities. Six strands are examined in this Study Arena:
- Interoperable Systems
- Network Capacity
- Facilities and Structures (FFE—Furniture Fixtures, and Equipment)
- IT Staffing
- IT Support Satisfaction
- Human Resource Management Systems

Optimal performance in Arena Three is Transformational (5.0)—Mobile Learning.

TIPS Performance Continuum Rubric—Arena Three

INFRASTRUCTURE AND FACILITIES					
STUDY ARENA THREE RESULTS →	**← PERFORMANCE CONTINUUM →**				
	Evolving (1.0–1.9)	**Developing (2.0–2.9)**	**Operational (3.0–3.9)**	**Innovative (4.0–4.9)**	**Transformational (5.0)**
	Proprietary	Fragmented	Consolidated System	Integrated Platforms	Mobile Learning
SUB-STRANDS ↓					
a. Interoperable Systems	Proprietary	Fragmented	Consolidated System	Integrated Platforms	Mobile Learning
b. Network Capacity	Limited Ethernet	Upgraded Ethernet	Unmanaged Wireless	Managed Wireless	Anytime, Anywhere Access
c. Facilities and Structure (FFE)	Antiquated	Existing Improvements	Capital Improvements	Strategic Roadmap	New Facilities
d. IT Staffing	Outsourced	Minimal	School Centric	Departmentalized	Proactive and Strategic
e. IT Support Satisfaction	Unresponsive	Minimal	Adequate	Responsive	Proactive and Strategic
f. Human Resources Management Systems	Paper Based	Separate Disparate Systems	Minimal Integration	HR Online Limited Integration	Integrated HR Management System

Interoperable Systems Strand (Arena Three)

Following are the TIPS ratings for the six sub-strands in this strand. *The descriptions of the ratings for each sub-strand in this table and the ones that follow have been omitted from this condensed report.*

TIPS Ratings—Interoperable Systems Strand (Arena Three)

INFRASTRUCTURE AND FACILITIES: Interoperable Systems					
SUB-STRANDS	**← PERFORMANCE CONTINUUM →**				
	Evolving (1.0–1.9)	Developing (2.0–2.9)	Operational (3.0–3.9)	Innovative (4.0–4.9)	Transformational (5.0)
(a-1) Application	1.0				
(a-2) Devices/Ratio		2.0			
(a-3) IT Platform Utilized		2.0			
(a-4) Delivery of Content			3.0		
(a-5) BYOD (Bring Your Own Device)		2.0			
(a-6) Current OS (Operating System)			3.0		

Network Capacity Strand (Arena Three)

Following are the TIPS ratings for the three sub-strands in this strand.

TIPS Ratings—Network Capacity Strand (Arena Three)

INFRASTRUCTURE AND FACILITIES: Network Capacity					
SUB-STRANDS	← PERFORMANCE CONTINUUM →				
	Evolving (1.0–1.9)	Developing (2.0–2.9)	Operational (3.0–3.9)	Innovative (4.0–4.9)	Transformational (5.0)
(b-1) User Access	1.0				
(b-2) Speed of Network		2.0			
(b-3) At Home Use	1.0				

Facilities and Structures Strand (Arena Three)

Following are the TIPS ratings for the four sub-strands in this strand.

TIPS Ratings—Facilities and Structures Strand (Arena Three)

INFRASTRUCTURE AND FACILITIES: Facilities and Structures					
SUB-STRANDS	← PERFORMANCE CONTINUUM →				
	Evolving (1.0–1.9)	Developing (2.0–2.9)	Operational (3.0–3.9)	Innovative (4.0–4.9)	Transformational (5.0)
(c-1) Ethernet				4.0	
(c-2) Electrical	1.0				
(c-3) Media Display			3.0		
(c-4) Classroom Furniture Structure				4.0	

IT Staffing Strand (Arena Three)

Following are the TIPS ratings for the two sub-strands in this strand.

TIPS Ratings—IT Staffing Strand (Arena Three)

INFRASTRUCTURE AND FACILITIES: IT Staffing					
SUB-STRANDS	← PERFORMANCE CONTINUUM →				
	Evolving (1.0–1.9)	Developing (2.0–2.9)	Operational (3.0–3.9)	Innovative (4.0–4.9)	Transformational (5.0)
(d-1) Personnel			3.0		
(d-2) Software Leads		2.0			

IT Support Satisfaction Strand (Arena Three)

Following are the TIPS ratings for the four sub-strands in this strand.

TIPS Ratings—IT Support Satisfaction Strand (Arena Three)

INFRASTRUCTURE AND FACILITIES: IT Support Satisfaction					
SUB-STRANDS	← PERFORMANCE CONTINUUM →				
	Evolving (1.0–1.9)	Developing (2.0–2.9)	Operational (3.0–3.9)	Innovative (4.0–4.9)	Transformational (5.0)
(e-1) Support for Teachers				4.0	
(e-2) Support for Parents	1.0				
(e-3) Support for Students				4.0	
(e-4) Surveys	1.0				

Arena Four: Resources

This arena measures the capacity of Central District and/or its district leadership team to provide the necessary accurate, on-time decisions, and the staff's motivation to understand, embrace, and support the district's vision, mission, and initiatives to actualize the vision into reality. Also supported in this arena is the capacity of the school/district to provide teachers and staff with the technical and digital resources necessary to support instruction and improve student achievement, as well as the accessibility to the appropriate tools that can address students' learning styles and needs through differentiated instruction.

TIPS team members met with focus groups and conducted individual interviews with the following participants to gather data for this Study Arena.

District Participants for Arena Four

FOCUS GROUP	INDIVIDUAL INTERVIEWS
Superintendent	Director—Technical Services
Assistant Superintendent	Human Resources Specialist
Director—Technical Services	Principal
Business Operations Manager	Curriculum Specialists (3)
Principals (2)	Teachers (2)
Teachers (3)	
EDC Lead	

The TIPS team members used the following TIPS Performance Continuum Rubric to measure the district's level of attainment for each strand of this arena and determine the overall rating for Arena Four—Resources. Three strands are examined in this Study Arena: 1) Personnel; 2) Financial; and 3) Instructional Content. Optimal performance in this arena is Transformational (5.0)—Seamless Integration.

TIPS Performance Continuum Rubric—Arena Four

RESOURCES					
STUDY ARENA FOUR RESULTS →	← **PERFORMANCE CONTINUUM** →				
	Evolving (1.0–1.9)	**Developing (2.0–2.9)**	**Operational (3.0–3.9)**	**Innovative (4.0–4.9)**	**Transformational (5.0)**
	Single Resources	Disparate	Minimal Integration	Limited Integration	Seamless Integration
STRANDS ↓					
a. Personnel	Minimal	School Centric	Outcome Model	Scalable and Cross Functional	Proactive and Strategic Partners
b. Finances	No resources linked to an initiative	Limited resources linked to an initiative	Adequate resources linked to an initiative	Resources tied to Central District Strategic Plan	All expenditures linked to Central District Strategic Plan
c. Instructional Content	Textbook Driven	Stand-alone Programs	Limited Technology Integration	Online Activities	Blended Learning Activities

To arrive at the rating for each strand, TIPS team members used evidence and gathered data to assign a numerical score to three process stages: Approach/Plan, Implementation, and Results. Combining the scores from the three process stages determined the total score for a strand. Based on the rubric, the total number of points for each strand could be as high as 15 or as low as 3 points. The following table shows the district's rating by strand in this arena. The highest possible cumulative score for this arena is 45 points. Supporting details for each of the numerical ratings cited in the following table are provided in greater detail in the following sections.

TIPS Ratings by Process Stages for Arena Four

RESOURCES				
STRAND	**PROCESS STAGES**			**STRAND TOTAL**
	APPROACH/ PLAN	**IMPLEMENTATION**	**RESULTS**	
a. Personnel	2.6	2.6	3.3	**8.5 of 15**
b. Finances	2.2	2.2	2.0	**6.4 of 15**
c. Instructional Content	2.0	1.2	1.0	**4.2 of 15**
Cumulative Score				**20.1 of 45**

Personnel Strand (Arena Four)

Measured within the strand of Personnel is the capacity of the district and/or district leadership team to provide the necessary accurate, on-time decisions and the capacity of the staff to understand, embrace, and support the district vision, mission, and initiatives to actualize the vision into reality. Following are the TIPS ratings that support this strand. *The detailed descriptions of each rating that would normally follow the table have been eliminated from this condensed report.*

TIPS Ratings—Personnel Strand (Arena Four)

RESOURCES: Personnel					
PROCESS STAGE	← **PERFORMANCE CONTINUUM** →				
	Evolving (1.0–1.9)	Developing (2.0–2.9)	Operational (3.0–3.9)	Innovative (4.0–4.9)	Transformational (5.0)
Approach/Plan		2.6			
Implementation		2.6			
Results			3.3		

Finances Strand (Arena Four)

Measured within the strand of Finances is the capacity of the school/district to access appropriate financial information and resources in order to provide the best service and support available to sustain teaching and learning. Following are the TIPS ratings that support this strand.

TIPS Ratings—Finances Strand (Arena Four)

RESOURCES: Finances					
PROCESS STAGE	← PERFORMANCE CONTINUUM →				
	Evolving (1.0–1.9)	Developing (2.0–2.9)	Operational (3.0–3.9)	Innovative (4.0–4.9)	Transformational (5.0)
Approach/Plan		2.2			
Implementation		2.2			
Results		2.9			

Instructional Content Strand (Arena Four)

Measured within the Instructional Content strand is the capacity of the school/district to provide teachers and staff with the resources to support education and improve student achievement. Teachers need access to the appropriate tools that will enable them to differentiate instruction for struggling students. Following are the TIPS ratings that support this strand.

TIPS Ratings—Instructional Content Strand (Arena Four)

RESOURCES: Instructional Content					
PROCESS STAGE	← PERFORMANCE CONTINUUM →				
	Evolving (1.0–1.9)	Developing (2.0–2.9)	Operational (3.0–3.9)	Innovative (4.0–4.9)	Transformational (5.0)
Approach/Plan		2.0			
Implementation	1.2				
Results	1.0				

Arena Five: Continuous Improvement

Measured within the Continuous Improvement arena is the capacity of the district and schools to systematically provide reliable assessments that can be used to determine strengths and opportunities for growth for all district initiatives, as well as staff and students. The data provided from these assessments should be accurate and available in real time. In addition, processes should be in place to use information obtained from data to develop or alter current practices to improve student learning.

TIPS team members met with focus groups and conducted individual interviews with the following participants to gather data for this Study Arena.

District Participants for Arena Five

FOCUS GROUP	INDIVIDUAL INTERVIEWS
Assistant Superintendent	Director—Technical Services
Director—Special Education	Curriculum Specialists (3)
School Psychologists (4)	Teachers (2)
Program Facilitators (2)	Teacher/Tutor

The TIPS team members used the following TIPS Performance Continuum Rubric to measure Central District's level of attainment for the one strand in this arena and determine the overall rating for Arena Five—Continuous Improvement. Optimal performance in this arena is Transformational (5.0)—Integrated.

TIPS Performance Continuum Rubric—Arena Five

CONTINUOUS IMPROVEMENT					
STUDY ARENA FIVE RESULTS →	← **PERFORMANCE CONTINUUM** →				
	Evolving (1.0–1.9)	**Developing (2.0–2.9)**	**Operational (3.0–3.9)**	**Innovative (4.0–4.9)**	**Transformational (5.0)**
	Isolation	Collected	Useable	Data Driven	Integrated
STRANDS ↓					
Progress Monitoring	Minimal monitoring and reporting of data	Data being collected	Data used to change current practices	Data collected and used on an ongoing basis to change current practices	Data-driven collaboration across all levels

To arrive at the rating for this strand, TIPS team members used evidence and gathered data to assign a numerical score to three process stages: Approach/Plan, Implementation, and Results. Combining the scores from the three process stages determined the total score for a strand. Based on the rubric, the total number of points for the strand could be as high as 15 or as low as 3 points. The following table shows the district's strand rating in this arena. The highest possible cumulative score for this arena is 15 points. *Supporting details have been omitted from this condensed report.*

TIPS Ratings by Process Stages for Arena Five

CONTINUOUS IMPROVEMENT				
STRAND	**PROCESS STAGES**			**STRAND TOTAL**
	APPROACH/ PLAN	**IMPLEMENTATION**	**RESULTS**	
Progress Monitoring	4.1	4.1	3.2	**11.4 of 15**

STUDY RECOMMENDATIONS

OVERALL FINDINGS

Based on the evidence and artifacts collected, the Commendations and Opportunities for Growth included in this section are intended to be beneficial in the district's implementation of its strategic goals and objectives. In addition, the retooling of some existing goals as well as the development of new ones can help drive future strategic planning, implementation, and monitoring for the highest-yielding results.

Below are the results of the TIPS: Technology Integration Planning Study™ on the Continuum for Technology Integration Planning. Each Study Arena has been assigned a measure of readiness. The level of readiness has been determined by calculating the mean score of the three Process Stages in Arenas One, Two, Three, and Five. Due to the nature of Study Arena Four, the mean score was determined by the readiness of each sub-stand rather than the process.

TIPS: Technology Integration Planning Study™

Performance Continuum By Measure					
STUDY ARENA	**DESCRIPTORS FOR EACH MEASURE**				
	EVOLVING (1.0–1.9).	**DEVELOPING** (2.0–2.9)	**OPERATIONAL** (3.0–3.9)	**INNOVATIVE** (4.0–4.9)	**EXEMPLARY** (5.0)
ONE Leadership and Decision Making	Autonomous	Systematized	*OUTCOME MODEL*	Transforma-tional	Sustainable Change
TWO Learning and Development for Teacher Effectiveness	Disconnected	Needs Dependent	*STANDARDS DRIVEN*	Student Centered	Personalized
THREE Infrastructure and Facilities	Proprietary	*FRAGMENTED*	Consolidated Systems	Integrated Platforms	Mobile Learning
FOUR Resources	Single Resources	Disparate	*MINIMAL INTEGRATION*	Limited Integration	Seamless Integration
FIVE Continuous Improvement	Isolation	Collected	Useable	*DATA DRIVEN*	Integrated